What people are saying about

Hothouse Utopia

The passage from radical theory to transformative practice may seem today more strewn with obstacles and bereft of guideposts than ever before. And yet, as Ryan Gunderson urges in his unsentimental account of "hothouse utopianism," the challenges we face in pursuing it should not lead us down the opposite path to quiescence and resignation. There are still genuine possibilities for transcending the status quo worth our efforts, despite everything, to realize their promise.

Martin Jay, Sidney Hellman Ehrman Professor Emeritus of History at the University of California, Berkeley, and author of *Reason After Its Eclipse: On Late Critical Theory* (2016) and *Splinters in Your Eye: Frankfurt School Provocations* (2020)

The possibility of dialectical thought has never been more hopeless, the need for it never more pressing. Revisiting the negative utopias of the Frankfurt School in the blood-red light of global ecological catastrophe, Gunderson works critical theory against the grain in a careful, painstaking effort to save philosophy from nihilism, hope from fatuity, and pessimism from despair. *Hothouse Utopia* is a timely, useful, and important contribution to the impossible yet necessary project of thinking a human future in the Anthropocene.

Roy Scranton, Associate Professor of English and Director of the Environmental Humanities Initiative at the University of Notre Dame, and author of *Learning to Die in the Anthropocene* (2015) and *We're Doomed. Now What?* (2018)

T0302779

Hothouse Utopia

Dialectics Facing Unsavable Futures

Ryan Gunderson

Hothouse Utopia

Dialectics Facing Unsavable Futures

Ryan Gunderson

Winchester, UK
Washington, USA

JOHN HUNT PUBLISHING

First published by Zero Books, 2021
Zero Books is an imprint of John Hunt Publishing Ltd., No. 3 East St., Alresford,
Hampshire SO24 9EE, UK
office@jhpbooks.com
www.johnhuntpublishing.com
www.zero-books.net

For distributor details and how to order please visit the 'Ordering' section on our website.

A CIP catalogue record for this book is available from the British Library.

Design: Stuart Davies

UK: Printed and bound by CPI Group (UK) Ltd, Croydon, CR0 4YY
Printed in North America by CPI GPS partners

We operate a distinctive and ethical publishing philosophy in
all areas of our business, from our global network of authors to
production and worldwide distribution.

Contents

Chapter 1 Doomed on All Fronts   1

Chapter 2 Alienated Reconciliation: Justify, "Act," Hide   32

Chapter 3 Three Flagellations of the Dialectic   73

Chapter 4 Utopianism Buried Between Catastrophes   95

Chapter 5 Anticipatory Reconciliation: Mere Possibility
          and Mundane Transcendence   118

Chapter 6 Hope in Negativity: Revolutionary Reformism
          Without Optimism   145

Previous titles

Gunderson R (2020) *Making the Familiar Strange: Sociology Contra Reification.* New York: Routledge. ISBN: 978-0367894429.

Stuart D, Gunderson R and Petersen B (2020) *The Degrowth Alternative: A Path to Address our Environmental Crisis?* New York: Routledge. ISBN: 978-0367894665.

Stuart D, Gunderson R and Petersen B (2020) *Climate Change Solutions: Beyond the Capital-Climate Contradiction.* Ann Arbor: University of Michigan Press. ISBN: 978-0472038473.

For Su. Even the darkest nights can't change who you are – the brightest, boldest, and roundest gem I've ever seen shining in this world. Thank you for coming into our family.

Acknowledgments

I would like to thank David Ashley, Claiton Fyock, and Diana Stuart for conversations related to themes developed throughout this book. Special thanks to Diana and Brian Petersen for helpful comments on an earlier draft. I would also like to thank William Attwood-Charles for reading recommendations, Stephen Lippmann for unknowingly titling the first chapter, and Jonathan Levy for unknowingly inspiring the imagined future slogan, "4°C is worse than 3°C!"

Some paragraphs and sections from chapters 3, 5, and 6 draw on:

Gunderson R (2015) A defense of the "Grand Hotel Abyss": The Frankfurt School's nonideal theory. *Acta Sociologica* 58(1): 25-38.

Gunderson R (2017) Ideology critique for the environmental social sciences: What reproduces the treadmill of production? *Nature and Culture* 12(3): 263-289.

Gunderson R (2018) Degrowth and other quiescent futures: Pioneering proponents of an idler society. *Journal of Cleaner Production* 198: 1574-1582.

Gunderson R (2020) Dialectics facing prehistoric catastrophe: Merely possible climate change solutions. *Critical Sociology* 46(4-5): 605-621.

Chapter 1

Doomed on All Fronts

Introduction: A searing sunrise

In a famous passage from the preface to the *Phenomenology of Spirit*, Hegel (1967: 75) calls periods like our own, "a birth-time, and a period of transition," where the:

> spirit of man has broken with the old order of things hitherto prevailing, and with the old ways of thinking, and is in the mind to let them all sink into the depths of the past and to set about his own transformation. ... [T]he spirit of the time, growing slowly and quietly ripe for the new form it is to assume, disintegrates one fragment after another of the structure of its previous world. That it is tottering to its fall is indicated only by symptoms here and there. Frivolity and again ennui, which are spreading in the established order of things, the undefined foreboding of something unknown— all these betoken that there is something else approaching. This gradual crumbling to pieces, which did not alter the general look and aspect of the whole, is interrupted by the sunrise, which, in a flash and at a single stroke, brings to view the form and structure of the new world.

Yet the generalized anxiety of our own age is not only caused by "undefined foreboding" that characterizes any period of rapid change, but, more distinctively, even the silver lining of birth-times, the sunrise previews into the new world, are blinding and burn the skin. Our sunrise is uncontrollable fires, more intense and pervasive heat waves, species extinctions, the spread of fascist-lite politics, facial-recognition technology, and

1

other trends that strike us as desirable as they are controllable.

We feel the weight of an old world crumbling while accelerating and bubbling full of unwelcoming possible futures. For similar though distinct historical reasons, Adorno opens *Negative Dialectics* with a dark rejoinder to Marx's eleventh thesis on Feuerbach— "Philosophers have hitherto only interpreted the world in various ways; the point is to change it"—by alluding to Hegel's other metaphor for periods of transition, that of pregnancy and birth.

> Philosophy, which once seemed obsolete, lives on because the moment to realize it was missed. The summary judgment that it had merely interpreted the world, that resignation in the face of reality had crippled it in itself, becomes a defeatism of reason after the attempt to change the world miscarried. (Adorno 1973a: 3)

Before exploring the meaning of this passage for dialectics today, let us first stare into our searing sunrise and inspect the swelling of another miscarriage of catastrophic proportions.

Political-economic trends and contradictions

Even after nearly half a century since its onset, it remains impossible to write a word about political-economic trends and contradictions of contemporary capitalism without discussing "neoliberalism." In response to the contradictions of the Keynesian-Fordist form of capitalism dominant from the Second World War into the 1970s, neoliberalism emerged as a political project to restore the power of the corporate and ruling classes against the relative political and economic power of organized workers and the welfare state (Harvey 2005). In theory, neoliberalism stresses individual freedom, especially to pursue free enterprise, and a state that promotes "strong individual private property rights, the rule of law, and the institutions of freely functioning markets and free trade" (Harvey 2005: 64). In practice, neoliberalism is associated with the deregulation of finance, more "flexible" labor markets (more part-time work, fewer benefits, weaker unions, etc.), reductions in social spending, the privatization of public goods and services, reductions in progressive taxes, and an overall business-friendly state. Neoliberalism as a political-economic program took hold in the 1970s in Chile after General Pinochet's murderous US- and CIA-backed coup and then found firm footing in the Reagan and Thatcher administrations in the US and UK, respectively. It has since become, and still is, the dominant global ideology of capitalism.

Peak neoliberalism is manifest in the US government's first organized response to the COVID-19 pandemic, where, amid skyrocketing unemployment and shortages in testing supplies and protective equipment, a $4.5 trillion corporate bailout was passed with little regulatory oversight along with a negligible single check for non-corporations (i.e., adult humans) (Carter 2020). Earlier, the Great Financial Crisis from 2007-2009 was an outcome of neoliberal policies as well as the structural transformation on which neoliberal ideology was erected: a transition from monopoly to monopoly-finance capitalism (Foster and Magdoff 2009). "Late" capitalism, ruled by giant monopolies, is necessarily marked by a lack of profitable investments in the "real" economy (overcapacity) and, thus, is increasingly reliant on debt and financial markets for investments. Finance, once tied to industry, has become a relatively autonomous feature of the economy (financialization). Monopoly-finance capital is marked by a prolonged period of stagnation, which, for the common person, means increased precariousness and inequality (Foster and McChesney 2012).

There are a few direct byproducts of neoliberal capitalism and its acceleration that concern us here: massive inequality, increased precariousness, and the rise of right-wing "populism."

First, massive inequality. The wealth gap between the top 5 percent and the bottom 90 percent of Americans has steadily increased since the dawn of neoliberalism (Wolff 2017). Here are just three statistics that capture the enormity of inequality in the US (see Inequality.org 2020):

- Three men own as much as the bottom half of Americans (Collins and Hoxie 2018).
- The richest 5 percent of Americans own two-thirds of the wealth (Wolff 2017).
- The top 1 percent and top 0.1 percent of Americans have more than doubled their wealth since 1983 (in 2016 dollars) while the total debts of the bottom 40 percent now exceed their assets ("negative wealth") (Wolff 2017).

Thanks in part to Occupy Wall Street (Gaby and Caren 2016), the problem of massive inequality has thrust itself into mainstream discourse. Yet, as Robinson (2019: 52ff) states in a clear summation of key indicators of US inequality, the average person does not comprehend the severity of inequality even if they are aware that society is unequal. Norton and Ariely (2011) found that most Americans want relatively egalitarian wealth distributions, and that actual wealth inequality is far greater than what they believe is the case. For example, respondents *believed* that the top 20 percent of the wealthiest Americans owned around 60 percent of the wealth but that they *should* own half that. The top 20 percent *actually* owns more than 80 percent of the wealth.

At the global level, wealth inequality is even more pronounced. One statistic communicates this clearly: eight men own the same amount of wealth as the poorest half of the world (3.6 billion people) (Oxfam 2017). Commentators like Bill Gates like to point out that global poverty has decreased while inequality has increased. However, if one picks a global poverty line that is higher than $2 a day—e.g., living on less than $7.40 a day—, the number of people living under the poverty line has increased (Hickel 2019).

Increased precariousness is massive inequality's bedfellow. I mean increased precariousness relative to the unionized manufacturing jobs of the Keynesian-Fordist period (cf. Kalleberg 2011).[1] In hindsight, the ability to afford a middle-class life working on a factory line during mid-twentieth century capitalism, with its "truce" between capital and labor, should be interpreted as an exception to, rather than the rule of, capitalist social relations. Today, as before this "Golden Age," those who need to work, work more, or work in better jobs are often faced with an inability to make enough money to buy commodities necessary for survival. The neoliberal "post-Fordist" economy is characterized by "flexible" labor markets of structural unemployment, underemployment, and involuntary part-time and/or temporary work. While I do not believe they are a new class (see Jonna and Foster 2016), Guy Standing's (2011) popular notion of *the precariat* helpfully captures the lives of many workers today, including difficulty in finding secure and stable work, low wages, no healthcare, weak or no union protection, irregular working times determined by the employer, and unsafe working conditions. However, even securing precarious employment is "lucky" relative to the global labor force, where over 60 percent of the available working population is inactive, unemployed, or vulnerably employed (e.g., rural subsistence workers), categories that do not even include temporary and part-time laborers (Jonna and Foster 2016).

The rise of right-wing "populism" is another political-economic byproduct of neoliberalism. Right-wing populism is a global tendency, including the administrations of Donald Trump in the US, Boris Johnson in the UK, Narendra Modi in India, Jair Bolsonaro in Brazil, Rodrigo Duterte in the Philippines, and Viktor Orbán in Hungary, the increasing popularity of right-wing populist parties throughout Europe (e.g., Alternative for Germany, the Swiss People's Party, and Marine Le Pen's National Rally/Front in France), and the 2019 coup against Evo Morales in Bolivia.

What does right-wing populism have to do with neoliberalism? First, neoliberalism as a political project has little ideological legitimacy today, and is widely viewed for what it is: a political project to redistribute wealth upwards (Harvey 2019). We are in the midst of the most pronounced legitimation crisis since the beginning of the end of the Keynesian welfare state (Habermas 1973). Today, the neoliberal project lives on *through* right-wing populist movements – neoliberalism is now in "an alliance with neo-fascism" (Harvey 2019).[2]

There is a second connection between neoliberalism and right-wing populism: the precarious conditions created by post-Fordism produces a desperation that powers right-wing populist movements and parties. Center-left parties, who ostensibly represent the common person, are responsible for pushing many of the neoliberal policies that put so many in desperate situations. In the US, the Democratic Party abandoned a mild social-democratic platform in favor of elite interests decades ago (Frank 2016). Yet the US is not unique here. In *Capital and Ideology* (2020), Thomas Piketty attempts to explain why, in the face of increasing inequality, people in the US, France, and the UK are turning to nativists instead of, as they did in the past, the left (for summary, see Schechter 2018). Based on voting behavior since the late 1940s, his thesis is that, beginning in the 1970s, center-left parties increasingly represented the interests of the "Brahmin Left" (the highly-educated elite) while the conservative parties continue to represent the "Merchant Right" (the traditional business elite). In contrast to the past, when voting behavior was primarily along class lines, now more educated citizens vote for the "Brahmin Left" parties while high-income and -wealth citizens vote for the "Merchant Right" parties. Both parties are detached from the interests of the common person, who, in an increasingly precarious situation, reacts against "the establishment," a disdain rising long before scapegoats like immigrants could be used to gain votes against the "globalists."

Piketty predicts, based on the 2016 elections in France and the US, that the future of political parties may be "globalist" parties (formerly center-left parties, self-described as "progressive") supported by higher-income and -education voters against "nativist" parties (right-wing populist, self-described as "patriotic") supported by lower-income and -education voters. The nativists of France, for example, secure working class support by framing the "progressive" globalists, with some accuracy, as "nomadic elites, without roots, always ready to squeeze workers and hire cheap immigrant labor," in contrast to the "patriotic" nativists who ostensibly "defend the interests of the less advantaged classes against the threats of hypercapitalist mongrelized globalization without borders or fatherland" (Piketty 2020: 797-798). While a social-democratic alternative has emerged in some countries, including the US (the movement surrounding Bernie Sanders), the UK (the movement surrounding Jeremy Corbyn), Germany (the movement surrounding Die Linke), Spain (the movement surrounding Podemos), and other countries, no alternative is large, organized, and powerful enough to turn society on a new track.

In summary, nearly a half century of neoliberalism has led to increases in precariousness, inequality, and reactionary politics. In capitalist societies, which subordinate life to abstract aims like profit-making and administrative goals, political-economic trends have a disproportionate influence on other social institutions, technological design and development, our psychology and identity, and the entire planet. While the rest of the trends and contradictions detailed below are not under the title "political-economic trends and contradictions," they can only be understood in the context of capitalism in general and post-Fordist capitalism in particular.

Technological contradictions and irrational technologies

Perhaps after skimming the news on one's smartphone — which, according to a 2016 market study, we "tap, type, swipe and click" 2,617 times a day (Winnick and Zolna 2016) — about the latest innovations in virtual reality, nanotechnology, artificial intelligence, military technology, biotechnology, and robotics, I suspect that one has, at some point, pondered if modern technology is a net good or net harm for humanity and the environment. One may have even wondered, with some embarrassment, if it would be better to live in a preindustrial society, a romanticism symptomatic of every anomic society (see below).

The dissonant feelings many feel toward technological civilization are captured by Freud in his *Civilization and Its Discontents* (1961: 34-35):

[d]uring the last few generations mankind has made an extraordinary advance in the natural sciences and in their technical application and has established his control over nature in a way never imagined before. ... Men are proud of those achievements, and have a right to be. But they seem to have observed that this newly-won power over space and time ... has not increased the amount of pleasurable satisfaction which they may expect from life and has not made them happier. ... One would like to ask: is there, then, no positive gain in pleasure, no unequivocal increase in my feeling of happiness, if I can, as often as I please, hear the voice of a child of mine who is living hundreds of miles away or if I can learn in the shortest possible time after a friend has reached his destination that he has come through the

long and difficult voyage unharmed? Does it mean nothing that medicine has succeeded in enormously reducing infant mortality and the danger of infection for women in childbirth, and, indeed, considerably lengthening the average life of a civilized man?

For thinkers such as Steven Pinker (2018), for whom the very meaning of progress is almost synonymous with technological innovation and economic growth, and sees contradictions in progress as blips that can be smoothly overcome, the answer is straightforward: of course there is a net gain in pleasure and happiness, and to say otherwise is romantic technophobia. In reply to this understandable affirmation of civilization:

> the voice of pessimistic criticism makes itself heard and warns us that most of these satisfactions follow the model of the "cheap enjoyment" extolled in the anecdote ... If there had been no railway to conquer distances, my child would never have left his native town and I should need no telephone to hear his voice; if travelling across the ocean by ship had not been introduced, my friend would not have embarked on his sea-voyage and I should not need a cable to relieve my anxiety about him. What is the use of reducing infantile mortality when ... we nevertheless rear no more children than in the days before the reign of hygiene, while at the same time we have created difficult conditions for our sexual life in marriage ...? And, finally, what good to us is a long life if it is difficult and barren of joys, and if it is so full of misery that we can only welcome death as a deliverer? (Freud 1961: 35)

There are two lines of thinking concerning technology, both associated with the Marxist tradition, helpful for explaining common dissonant attitudes toward technology while avoiding the well-known pitfalls of romantic primitivism, on the one hand, and the naïve techno-optimism of those who turn a blind eye to the contradictory impacts of technological progress, on the other. First, sometimes the potential positive impacts of technology are "fettered"—blocked or underexploited—due to existing social relations and, second, technological design and use "embodies" or "materializes" existing social relations. I discuss each argument in turn.

The first line of argument—that some technological artifacts could be used for more rational ends if embedded in different social conditions is most famously expressed in Marx's notion of the contradiction between the forces and relations of production. Humans have enslaved themselves to techniques that could free them from unnecessary toil. Thinking about the rationality and goodness of technological use as contingent on existing social relations helps evade the blind spots of both technophobia and techno-optimism as well as clarify today's technological contradictions. For example, we currently have the technological ability to reduce greenhouse gas emissions given different social conditions and priorities, but, instead, we are constantly increasing total energy use, including fossil fuel-based energy (Gunderson et al. 2018; York and Bell 2019). The question, returned to in chapter 5, remains the same: Will we become slaves to our own technics or use them for rational aims?

The case that there is a contradiction between the forces and relations of production assumes that technological development and use are social, not neutral and inevitable. This is also assumed in the second Marxist claim about technology, that it "embodies" the social order and its ideology. This argument is at least as old as Marx (Malm 2018), an insight later expanded by thinkers such as Herbert Marcuse (1964) and Erich Fromm (1968), and, more recently, by Andrew Feenberg (1999) and Adam Greenfield (2017). In short, the goals of profit-maximization and cost-effectiveness condition the design and use of many technologies: "design embodies only a subset of the values circulating in society at any given time" and capitalism is unique in that the range of possible value-mediations of technology are reduced due to "conflict[s] with a narrow pecuniary interest" (Feenberg 2005: 105). If this is true, that technology is shaped by social conditions, this also means that, if we assume that some social conditions are irrational, there may be some technological artifacts that would remain irrational even if embedded in a rational society. That is, there may be technologies that would be made unnecessary or actively abolished by a rational society. For example, "[w]hat sense would it make to try to turn the assembly line into a scene of self-expression, or to broadcast propaganda for free thought" (Feenberg 2005: 98)? Such "irrational technologies," for want of a better term, not only serve destructive and repressive ends in the current order, but also, due to their design, are inherently antithetical to human flourishing and ecological wellbeing.

Before shrugging off this line of argument—that some technologies are inherently destructive and could never serve rational ends—as technophobic, consider two concrete examples of contemporary irrational technologies: facial-recognition technology and stratospheric aerosol injection (SAI).

It is easy to envision frightening future worlds with the spread of facial-recognition software.

One worries what happens when facial-recognition technology improves and proliferates ever further, enabling relative conveniences like Amazon's automated brick-and-mortar stores while ensuring that people can be identified, by a host of unknown actors, wherever they go. One dark scenario is the "Minority Report" option, as in the film where public advertisements, cameras, and sensors scan Tom Cruise's eyes and provide him with personalized offers and ads wherever he goes, with advertising flowing from one interface to another. (Silverman 2017: 159)

[W]hen walking down a city street, we still tend to nurture the unconscious assumption that we are somehow insulated in our privacy by the others surrounding us. But the advent of powerful facial-recognition algorithms, and particularly the escape of those algorithms from their original context, threatens our ability to remain anonymous in this way—and by extension, our ability to assemble in public, demonstrate collective grievances and assert popular power. (Greenfield 2017: 240)

Yet these nightmarish scenarios are not far-off fictional dystopias. In the case of the Minority Report dystopia, Silverman (2017: 159) continues, "[m]uch of this technology already exists, and advertisers are focused on tracking users wherever they go, including across devices, and (by closely tracking behaviors) distinguishing between multiple users sharing the same device" (Silverman 2017: 159). And following the problem of maintaining anonymity, Greenfield (2017: 241f) notes that FindFace, an application available in Russia, already allows users to upload pictures of strangers, which it compares with hundreds of millions of users of Russia's major social networking site VKontakte. Although the Chinese state is currently at the forefront of frightening applications of facial-recognition technology, there are concerning parallel trends in the West (Wong and Dobson 2019). For example, a recent *New York Times* exposé details how a previously obscure and unregulated tech startup, Clearview AI, has amassed an enormous database of billions upon billions of photographs and images milled from the internet without consent (Hill 2020). Law enforcement agencies pay to access this database to compare suspect photos. Matches are provided with links to the webpages from which the photos were extracted.

While facial-recognition software could serve the rulers of any repressive society, it should currently be examined in the context of "surveillance capitalism." Surveillance is a necessary feature of every mechanism monopoly capitalist societies have adopted to absorb excess surplus since the Second World War: military expansion, marketing, and, with the dawn of neoliberalism, financialization (Foster and McChesney 2014). The capacity to monitor entire populations entered a new era with information technologies. According to Shoshana Zuboff (2015: 75, 76), surveillance capitalism is a "new logic of accumulation" that "aims to predict and modify human behavior as a means to produce revenue and market control" as well as turning everyday life into a "commercialization strategy" (cf. Greenfield 2017). The "raw material" of surveillance capitalism is behavioral data, which is accumulated as a "behavioral surplus" that is used, via machine intelligence, to predict what people will do in the future in order to sell them products, creating "behavioral futures markets" (Zuboff 2019: 9). For Facebook, facial-recognition technology opens "infinite" marketing possibilities and, thus, they actively fight against laws to regulate facial recognition (Zuboff 2019: 251ff). This new logic of accumulation in which, for example, Google "extracts" voice samples, emails, online search histories, smartphone location data, etc., without consent, allows the firm to undermine the real or illusionary past "structural reciprocities between the firm and its populations" and makes way for an emerging form of absolute power: a totally controlled and constantly monitored world of automaton-like humans who exist as a "hive mind" from which there is "no escape" (Zuboff 2015: 80, 2019: chs. 16 and 17).

To provide another example of inherently irrational and destructive technics, consider plans for solar geoengineering, strategies to reflect incoming solar radiation back into space (US National Research Council 2015). SAI, the most widely discussed form of solar geoengineering, is a plan to emulate volcanism by releasing particles into the stratosphere to increase albedo (Keith 2013). While cheap compared to carbon emissions reductions (mitigation) and potentially effective at cooling the planet, SAI is extremely risky, as emphasized even by scientists who support more SAI research (e.g., Keith 2013). Risks include unknown impacts on weather, clouds, and plants; the potential for more severe and frequent droughts; increases in air pollution and acid rain; potential to worsen the ozone hole; problems resulting from possible military use or commercial control; and, most frighteningly, the possibility for a "termination effect," where, if SAI cannot be maintained after being implemented, temperatures could increase rapidly due to a build-up of background emissions (see Robock 2008a, 2008b, Robock et al. 2009, Robock et al. 2010; Boucher et al. 2013, Ferraro et al. 2014).

Like facial-recognition technology, SAI is difficult to understand without political-economic context. While solar geoengineering scientists who support SAI research push for increasing mitigation efforts and are usually cautious about their support (Reynolds et al. 2016), there is partial though illuminating evidence that SAI may be implemented in order to reproduce capitalism, the social order that drives climate change (Gunderson et al. 2019). Not only are economic justifications for SAI common (e.g., unlike mitigation, SAI does not immediately threaten industry), which will appeal to those with the power to implement climate policy, but there is some evidence of support for SAI from the elite (e.g., Bill Gates), fossil fuel industry representatives, and even climate denialist organizations (e.g., the Heartland Institute) because it is perhaps the only potentially "effective" climate change strategy, the catastrophic risks be damned, that is simultaneously "economical" and capable of reproducing the status quo (Ott 2018; Surprise 2018; Gunderson et al. 2019; Foster 2019).

Both facial-recognition technology and SAI are examples of

technologies that, embedded in current social conditions, "leave existing modes of domination mostly intact" (Greenfield 2017: 8). Yet the point of labeling them "irrational technologies" here is to ask the reader to reflect on the following question: Can or will either technology "ever truly be turned to liberatory ends" (Greenfield 2017: 8)? It is difficult to imagine social conditions in which the capacity to compare a photograph of someone's face with billions of face-photographs, which were likely obtained and stored without consent, would increase human flourishing.[3] What use would a non-repressive society have for such an *inherently* repressive technic of arbitrary power? Similarly, a rational society, which would immediately and dramatically reduce carbon emissions, would never conceive of implementing SAI. Only an irrational society would inject millions of tons of sulfate aerosols into the stratosphere rather than reduce emissions.

There are many emerging and rapidly developing technologies that should be subjected to similar analysis: Are they only destructive due to the social conditions in which they are embedded or are they inherently destructive, regardless of social conditions? But most of us on a typical day would prefer to look away from such troubling questions. Fear of the future due to rapid technological change— "future shock" (Toffler 1970)—is one of the rots on which despair spores.

Despair, anomie, and alienation

With over a century to digest Nietzsche and Freud, it should not surprise us that there is widespread despair in a society that insists upon individual happiness:

- Around 1 in 6 American adults took a psychiatric drug in 2013 (Moore and Mattison 2017).
- Nearly 1 in 5 American adults had a mental illness in 2017 (National Institute of Mental Health 2019).

- Nearly *half* of American adolescents aged 13-18, including the *majority* of girls, had a mental health disorder between 2001-2004 (Merikangas et al. 2010).
- The national suicide rate increased by 24 percent from 1999 through 2014 (Curtin et al. 2016).
- 19.7 million Americans aged 12 or older had a substance use disorder in 2017 (Substance Abuse and Mental Health Services Administration 2018).
- 70,237 Americans died from drug overdoses in 2017, 47,600 of these deaths involved opioids (National Institution on Drug Abuse 2019).

The COVID-19 pandemic accelerated these trends. A poll conducted by the Centers for Disease Control and Prevention in June 2020 found that 4 in 10 respondents reported at least one of the following: "symptoms of anxiety disorder or depressive disorder (30.9%), symptoms of a trauma- and stressor-related disorder (TSRD) related to the pandemic (26.3%), and having started or increased substance use to cope with stress or emotions related to COVID-19 (13.3%)" (Czeisler et al. 2020). Astonishingly, a *quarter* of respondents aged 18-24 reported that they had *seriously considered suicide* in the past 30 days.

Data points like these are difficult to interpret for those raised in a society that individualizes problems such as mental illness. (In fact, there is even a campaign that we increase our "acceptance" of mental health issues, as opposed to altering the social conditions that produced the mental health crisis.) Of course, biographical, psychological, and/or genetic variables are indispensable for explaining individual cases of mental health issues, suicides, and drug abuse, but these micro-level variables cannot explain such high *rates* of mental health issues, suicides, and drug abuse. The goal of this section is not to make the extravagant claim that capitalism is responsible for all mental health issues, suicides, and overdoses, but, instead, to point out that these trends are incomprehensible without zooming out to see their social context.

There are connections between capitalism, especially in its neoliberal form, and mental health issues, drug abuse, and other indicators of despair. The *normal* processes of capitalism, such as brutal competition, materialism, inequality, and self-interested pseudo-individualism, create the richest soil to grow mental pathologies in individuals (Fisher 2009; Verhaeghe 2014; Monbiot 2016; Tweedy 2017; Kovel 2018; Matthews 2020). For example, perceived and experienced job insecurity and poverty are associated with increased risk for mental illness (Marmot et al. 2001; Sverke et al. 2002; Lund et al. 2010) and there is increasing evidence that income inequality is a driver of various mental illnesses, drug abuse, and related issues (Wilkinson and Pickett 2010; Burns 2015). The political-economic forces conditioning mental health issues, suicide, and drug abuse are clearest in Case and Deaton's (2015) well-known paper on "deaths of despair": a dramatic increase in mortality rates since 1999 among white middle-aged Americans without a college degree. The likely underlying cause in increased mortality rates driven by suicide and drug and alcohol abuse is simple: a lack of good jobs (Case and Deaton 2017). Indicators of despair can even remain for portions of the population whose basic needs are met. For example, relatively high substance use and mental health issues of children of affluent parents may be caused by emotional and physical isolation from parents as well as familial and internalized obsession with achievement (Luthar 2003; Luthar and Becker 2003).

What also needs explaining is the generalized anxiety of our era even when it does not manifest or morph into substance abuse, depression, suicide, and other "maladjustments." There are two classical sociological concepts that shed light: *alienation* and *anomie*.

Alienation is a Hegelian term usurped by the young Marx

(1964) to describe the state of being dominated by one's own material and immaterial artifacts, of a world created by humans becoming an alien force, a condition epitomized by wage labor, where humans are alienated from their product, productive activity, species being, and fellow humans. Alienation is unfreedom, an unfreedom created and reproduced by the very authors who desire to be free. Although alienation is a term used to describe an objective condition of a world of subjects dominated by their own artifacts, it is the *lived* world of the subject that is estranged. Freudo-Marxists like Marcuse and Fromm argue that the alienation caused by the instrumental rationalization of production and leisure, which stifles creativity, cooperation, and freedom, was at the center of modern mental illness (see Matthews 2020). Fromm (1955) argues that mental health issues are common in affluent capitalist societies because, even when the basic needs of citizens are met, individuals are encouraged to meet their "existential needs," such as a sense of identity, unity, and relatedness to others, in pathological ways. For example, consumer capitalism conditions a ubiquitous "marketing character," a personality type that experiences the world and the self as a commodity. One must sell their fluid and pseudo-cheerful "personality package" at work and fulfill the need for meaning through consumption and shopping. Yet, for Fromm, even the normal processes of capitalism are a collective insanity. For example, food production and distribution are restricted to save "the economy" despite the reality of malnourishment; there are high rates of education, literacy, and a massive infrastructure of advanced communicative technology coupled with increased leisure, yet most time free from wage labor is spent consuming childish entertainment; and poverty and homelessness continue to exist in the face of abundance and empty homes.

In addition to alienation, our society is also characterized by what the great French sociologist Émile Durkheim terms "anomie."[4] Anomie simultaneously describes normless social conditions following rapid social changes and the psychological state Durkheim (1951: 369, 247) thought normative in these periods: a "collective sadness" and "constantly renewed torture" formed by an "[i]nextinguishable thirst" that roams free of any concrete and attainable goals. It is the collective ennui and "undefined foreboding of something unknown" (Hegel 1967: 75) mentioned in the opening lines of this book. Chris Hedges (2018) skillfully applies Durkheim's concept to diagnose today's despair and cultural pathologies that he believes foreshadow the collapse of the American empire. While the following claim is difficult to corroborate empirically, there seems to be a robust sense, especially among young people, that the current era is culturally barren and morally bankrupt, that one cannot locate a solid frame of reference to orient one's self, that life is "out of control" and irrational, and that the future is unwelcoming if not inevitably disastrous. This is anomie, manifest today in the nostalgia for past cultural forms, the bored yet hurried pace through which one skims the ever-expanding cosmos of algorithmically-selected digital "infotainment," a craving for unshakable certainties (a necessarily fruitless search terminating in skepticism or dogmatism), the fleeting hope that shopping will rid one of a nagging desire rather than producing a new one (Meštrović 1991), and the dread in imagining a future world where emerging trends such as surveillance technology and wristbands that track movements at work are so familiar and ubiquitous that they are as taken-for-granted as toaster ovens and advertising.

As with past metamorphoses in capitalism, the underlying social relations that drive technological and cultural change are reproduced and strengthened through these changes. In other words, the most essential roles and dynamics of capitalist society stay the same despite capitalism's unique ability to constantly transform itself. I suspect that contemporary anomie is partly caused by the end of the legitimacy of the neoliberal project even though it continues to guide the state and economy (Harvey 2019). This strain between ideology and social contradictions produces a feeling that "the old is dying and the new cannot be born," a tension that forms "a great variety of morbid symptoms" (Gramsci 1971: 276; see Fraser 2019). While our morbid symptoms include the use of authoritarian power rather than consent to rule, as Gramsci predicted, the most unnerving experience feeding neoliberal anomie is knowledge that the new world that must be born will likely be catastrophic.

Ecological destruction

A 2015 *Science* article outlines nine "planetary boundaries" that, when crossed, may threaten the ability of Earth to maintain a "safe operating space" for social development (Steffen et al. 2015). Of the planetary boundaries that can be quantified, we are already in the "zone of uncertainty" of "increasing risk" for climate change and land-system change, and "beyond the zone of uncertainty" of "high risk" for biosphere integrity, specifically genetic diversity and biogeochemical flows. Here, I focus on two already-crossed planetary boundaries: biodiversity loss and climate change.

Genetic diversity is necessary for the biosphere to adapt to long-term changes yet human activity, such as the basic processes of capitalist expansion, is rapidly wiping out many species and using ecosystems unsustainably. For example, the World Wildlife Federation (2016) estimates a 58 percent decline in vertebrates since 1970. That is, *over half* of vertebrate populations have been terminated since the transition from Keynesian to neoliberal capitalism. In fact, the Millennium Ecosystem Assessment (2005: 1) found that "[o]ver the past 50 years, humans have changed ecosystems more rapidly and extensively than in any comparable period of time in human history" and that 60 percent of ecosystem "services" are "being degraded or used unsustainably." The current extinction rate is interpreted as high risk because of uncertainty about when biodiversity loss will "trigger non-linear or irreversible changes to the Earth system" (Steffen et al. 2015: 1259855-6).

If the current impacts of climate change caused by around 1°C warming above preindustrial levels only constitute an "increasing risk," what would pushing this planetary boundary into "high risk" look like? The goal of the 2015 Paris Climate Agreement of the 21st Conference of the Parties of the United Nations Framework Convention on Climate Change (2015) is "keeping a global temperature rise this century well below 2 degrees Celsius above pre-industrial levels and to pursue efforts to limit the temperature increase even further to 1.5 degrees Celsius." A recent Special Report of the Intergovernmental Panel on Climate Change (IPCC), *Global Warming of 1.5°C* (2018; for readable overview, see Buis 2019), details reasons why a 1.5°C warmer world would be much less risky and undesirable than a 2°C warmer world, including lower mean temperatures in most regions, fewer hot extremes in most inhabited regions, a lower probability of drought in some regions, lower sea-level rise, less biodiversity loss, and fewer health, food, water, security, and other risks to humans. The social and ecological forecasts of a 2°C world are grim, including:

- 37 percent of Earth's population exposed to severe heatwaves at least once every 5 years.
- "The deadly heatwaves India and Pakistan saw in 2015 may occur annually" (Buis 2019).
- The coldest nights in high latitudes will be about 6°C warmer.
- Increased amount, intensity, and/or frequency in heavy precipitation, increased flooding and runoff in most areas, and heavier rainfall from tropical cyclones.
- A less secure food supply, including areas that are already very poor such as the African Sahel and Western

and Southern Africa.

- 13 percent of land areas are "projected to see their ecosystems shift from one type of biome to another" (e.g., a land-area covered in rainforest shifting to a new form of vegetation) (Buis 2019).
- The potential of thawing 1.5 to 2.5 million square kilometers of currently frozen permafrost.
  - Arctic permafrost contains 1.8 trillion tons of carbon, twice as much as there is currently in the Earth's atmosphere, much of which will be released as methane, a greenhouse gas far more potent than carbon dioxide (Wallace-Wells 2017).
- The climatically determined geographic range of 18 percent of the insects, 16 percent of the plants, and 8 percent of the vertebrates will be reduced by more than half.
- More than 70 percent of the Earth's coastlines will experience sea-level rise greater than 0.2 meters, increasing salinization of water supplies, beach erosion, and coastal flooding.
- Increased ocean acidification, leading to the loss of almost all coral reefs (> 99 percent).
- An ice-free Arctic Ocean once a decade.

The IPCC (2018: 21, 17) emphasizes that societies would need to fundamentally and immediately alter the status quo to remain within 1.5°C warming: "rapid and far-reaching transitions in energy, land, urban and infrastructure, and industrial systems" are required, changes that are "unprecedented in terms of scale."

How close is society to making these "unprecedented" and "far-reaching" changes to combat climate change? Not close at all. Climate scientists Kevin Anderson and Alice Bows (2011: 41) predicted that there is "little to no chance" of even staying within

2°C, which they consider the border between "dangerous" and "extremely dangerous" climate change. According to Climate Analytics, a think tank that tracks the emissions and climate policies of over 32 countries that produce around 80 percent of total emissions, only two countries, Morocco and the Gambia, are on track to keeping global temperature rise within 1.5°C warming (Climate Action Tracker 2019). In fact, even if all countries achieved all of their current pledges and targets, which is highly unlikely, we can expect temperature increases of 3.5°C (Climate Action Tracker 2019). This is well-above catastrophic range. There is high confidence that 3°C warming relative to preindustrial levels would result in extensive biodiversity loss, very high risks to unique and threatened systems, and high risk of "large and irreversible sea level rise from ice sheet loss" (IPCC 2014: 72). Earth has not been that hot for around 3 million years, during the Pliocene Epoch, an epoch that the director of NASA's Goddard Institute for Space Studies, Gavin Schmidt, describes as a time where "there was almost no ice anywhere. The sea level was 20 meters (65 feet) or so higher, and forests went to the edge of the Arctic Ocean where there is now tundra … It takes a long time for those changes to manifest, but if we see 3 C … it pushes us in that direction" (quoted in Lewis 2015).

If countries do not achieve all their current pledges and continue with current policies, Climate Action Tracker (2019) predicts a temperature rise of 2.3°C to 4.1°C above preindustrial levels by 2100. Thankfully warming above 4°C is less likely than previously estimated, though this depends on future coal use (International Energy Agency 2019; Wallace-Wells 2019b) and potential warming-induced feedbacks (Steffen et al. 2018; see below). However, it is important to examine risks related to higher-end projections. Risks of a 4°C or warmer world "include severe and widespread impacts on unique and threatened systems, the extinction of many species, large risks to food security and compromised normal human activities, including growing food or working outdoors in some areas for parts of the year, due to the combination of high temperature and humidity" (IPCC 2014: 65).

The World Bank's *Turn Down the Heat: Why a 4°C Warmer World Must be Avoided* (2012) is devoted to projecting the possible future hell of a 4°C warmer world, including:

- Extreme heat waves becoming the "new normal."
- "In regions such as the Mediterranean, North Africa, the Middle East, and the Tibetan plateau, almost all summer months are likely to be warmer than the most extreme heat waves presently experienced" (World Bank 2012: xv).
- A 150 percent increase in ocean acidity, a concentration likely unparalleled in Earth's history.
- 0.5 to 1 meter average sea-level rise (highly asymmetrical based on region).
- A significant exacerbation of water scarcity in many regions, especially "northern and eastern Africa, the Middle East, and South Asia, while additional countries in Africa would be newly confronted with water scarcity on a national scale due to population growth" (World Bank 2012: xvi).
- Increased risks of "ecosystem disruption" due to extreme weather events like wildfires, forest dieback, and ecosystem transformation and shifts.
- Difficulty with adequate food output due to the increased prevalence and intensity of drought and other factors, such as seawater penetration of aquifers (e.g., Bangladesh, Egypt, and Vietnam).

In the words of Anderson, a 4°C warmer world is "incompatible with an organized global community, is likely to be beyond 'adaptation', is devastating to the majority of ecosystems, and has a high probability of not being stable" (quoted in Roberts 2011).

Yet global average temperatures could exceed 4°C above preindustrial levels by the end of the century, pushing upwards from 5°C—the worst-case median projection of the IPCC's (2014) Fifth Assessment Report—to 7°C (see Hood 2019). These are the terrifying possible-yet-unlikely futures David Wallace-Wells focuses on in his controversial "The uninhabitable Earth" (2017), a work based on scientific research supplemented with interviews with climate scientists. To only provide a few examples:

- In a 5°C warmer world there may be 50 percent less grain despite 50 percent more people.
- In a 6°C warmer world, "the Earth's ecosystem will boil with so many natural disasters that we will just start calling them 'weather'" and, in the summer, "everybody in the country east of the Rockies would be under more heat stress than anyone, anywhere, in the world today."
- In a 7°C warmer world, one would be "cooked to death from both inside and out" within a few hours of being in a Costa Rican jungle on a 105°F day.

The most unnerving climate change study to date is Steffen et al.'s (2018) argument that even if societies manage to keep global warming within 1.5-2°C of preindustrial levels, Earth may cross a planetary boundary in which global average temperatures stabilize at 4-5°C higher than preindustrial temperatures due to numerous carbon cycle feedbacks caused by warming. Warming-induced feedbacks, such as permafrost loss and forest dieback, would increase greenhouse gas emissions and project the planet into an irreversible "Hothouse Earth," which "is likely to be uncontrollable and dangerous to many, particularly if we transition into it in only a century or two, and it poses severe risks for health, economies, political stability (especially for the most climate vulnerable), and ultimately, the habitability of the planet for humans" (Steffen et al. 2018: 8256). In other words, even staying below 2°C, which is highly unlikely, puts us at risk for runaway catastrophic warming.

Climate change is driven by the basic processes of capitalism. Capitalism must expand to survive due to competition and other mechanisms, and perpetual growth increases carbon emissions (Foster et al. 2010; Antonio and Clark 2015; Klein 2015). The system is in an accelerating process of "creative self-destruction" (Wright and Nyberg 2015), and is now constituted by a suicidal contradiction between capital's need to expand and accelerate production, on the one hand, and the destructive effects expansionistic, accelerated production has on the conditions of production, specifically the climate system, on the other (Stuart et al. 2020a). The centrality of the neoliberal form of capitalism driving climate change becomes clear when considering the percentage of total carbon emissions that have occurred in just the last 3 decades: more than half (Wallace-Wells 2017). While technocrats deny this contradiction by promising "green growth" and other impossibilities (see chapter 2), global carbon emissions and temperatures continue to rise, save a relatively sharp recent reduction in emissions due to COVID-19's economic slowdown.

Those who will be most negatively impacted by climate change, including catastrophic climate change, are those who have done the least to cause climate change: the poorest areas in the world (e.g., World Bank 2012; Harlan et al. 2015). For example, projections show significantly higher sea-level rise in the tropics, increased tropical cyclone intensity in low-latitude regions, and increased drought in tropical and subtropical regions – all disproportionately poor areas (World Bank 2012). As stressed in Naomi Klein's *On Fire* (2019), perhaps the greatest climate injustice that is already emerging is the ruthlessness with which climate refugees from poor countries who have done comparatively little to contribute to carbon emissions, are being "dealt with" by many core countries, countries responsible for the majority of carbon emissions.

Of all the trends and contradictions discussed above that point to the likelihood of a catastrophic "miscarriage" in the future, I give the most attention throughout the rest of the book to the ecological crisis, especially climate change, because I think it is the most serious threat facing twenty-first century earthlings, human and nonhuman. A second reason I focus on the ecological crisis is that it is a material counterpoint to the typical liberal reply that "All is well" to leftist critiques of the status quo, a reply condensed in a quip from Pinker's popular *Enlightenment Now* (2018: 39): "[i]ntellectuals who call themselves 'progressive' *really* hate progress." There are undeniable material gains of the modern era. This is not in dispute. But, as Robinson (2019: 47) says, when evaluating the justness and rationality of the present, it makes more sense to compare what is actual to what is possible than it does to compare what is actual to what was. As detailed throughout the book, comparing the actual to the potential is fundamental to dialectical thinking. Further, rather than showing that fewer people are poorer than they were a century or two ago—a claim that assumes, for example, that former peasants who used to grow their own food are now better off living as wage laborers in slums (Hickel 2019)—, a far more important and honest task is explaining the necessary entanglement of regression and destruction in what we term "progress" and "rationality." For example, what is starkly missing in accounts like Pinker's defense of progress is the absolute ecological devastation *caused* by "progress," including climate change, increases in dead zones, the rapid rate of species extinctions, dramatic drops in freshwater resources per capita, etc. (see Lent 2018). One task of thinking today is to make sure that this level of destruction is seen as a *constitutive* rather than an accidental feature of capitalist "development" and "progress." The ability to see how irrationality is bound up with what is currently considered rational does not undermine the enlightenment, but, instead, points to the possibility of a truer progress and more rational rationality (Horkheimer and Adorno 1969). This is still the task of dialectical thinking today.

Book purpose and outline: From systems and trends to experience and thought

Even a brief exploration of political-economic trends, destructive technological innovations, the ubiquity of despair, and the constantly accelerating assault on the planet reinforces what the reader already knows; we live in scary times and the future is potentially catastrophic. And the above brief tour does not touch on the risk of nuclear war, inequalities in education and healthcare, a criminal justice system that ruins millions of lives, racial and gender inequality, the continued intensification of agricultural practices—including the brutal treatment of billions and billions of defenseless animals—, and other areas of concern. However, this book is less about systemic contradictions than it is about the experience of systemic contradictions, and how to position consciousness against them. To return to Hegel's metaphor of rapid social change as experienced in collective fear of the future with some glimpses of the new world in a sunrise, this book is not about our scorching sunrise itself, sketched above, but, instead, the modes of action and thought through which we react to its sweltering light and how we can productively sustain the search for a livable future against all odds.

This book evolved as a response to a distressing question that plagues anyone who desires to make the world a better place: What if we fail? This conundrum takes on an alarming significance in the age of climate change because we cannot afford to fail if the future is to be habitable. Yet continuing climate inaction seems much more likely than a global ecological transition. While this book examines concrete political opportunities to address the climate crisis, that is not its central aim and is a topic I have addressed elsewhere (e.g., Stuart et al. 2020a). Instead, an underlying goal is to explore the implications of the likelihood of continual failure for the possibility of envisioning, let alone building, a rational society.

To explore the significance of the risk of climate catastrophe for the utopian spirit, I have found the work of "critical" or "Western" Marxists, Theodor W. Adorno and Ernst Bloch in particular, to be invaluable (for intellectual history, see Jay 1982). In comparison to Soviet or "scientific" Marxism, Western Marxism is more attentive to the dynamics of ideology and culture, not to supplant traditional political-economic questions or to abandon a historical materialist framework, but, instead, to get a better grasp on the problem of *social reproduction*. Especially for a group of unorthodox Marxists associated with Frankfurt, Germany's Institute of Social Research ("the Frankfurt School"), the questions of why humans continue to accept an alienated existence rather than form a rational society became paramount with the rise of consumer-monopoly capitalism, Stalinism, and fascism (see chapter 3). The challenge of these pesky questions for the left has only snowballed with the ecological crisis, and the Western Marxist tradition provides a helpful framework, drawn on and explicated throughout the book, for explanation and reflection (cf. Stoner and Melathopoulos 2015).

Chapter 2 examines modes of action and thought through which people attempt to reconcile themselves with a contradictory world in ways that reproduce the social conditions that produced the desire for reconciliation, counterproductive flights from chaos I call "alienated reconciliation." There are at least three overarching forms of alienated reconciliation: (1) justify systemic contradictions, (2) take ineffective "action" against systemic contradictions, actions that paradoxically reproduce rather than challenge the social order, and (3) try to shield one's consciousness from systemic contradictions by pursuing various forms of escapism.

Dialectical thinking is the alternative to reconciling oneself with the status quo. Dialectics is a form of thought that uncovers systemic contradictions and looks for potential futures already present in these contradictions. Chapter 3 explains three setbacks suffered by the dialectic since Hegel and early Marxism: (1) a loss of faith in the inevitability of the realization of human freedom through the inner workings of history; (2) a lack of confidence in a historical subject to bring about the potential for a better future; and, most recently, (3) the undermining of an essential prerequisite for the possibility of human freedom: a livable life environment. The goal of this book is to keep dialectics afloat in the wake of these discouragements.

Chapter 4 explores the prospects for a rational search for utopia, the sometimes-implicit underlying aim of dialectical thought, despite being temporally surrounded by two catastrophes: the past catastrophe of human history and the likelihood of future catastrophic climate change. Even though we cannot redeem the past and can no longer save the future, I argue that utopian thought is salvageable because we can still rationally hope for a less bad future.

Chapter 5 identifies concrete possibilities for a less bad future, focusing on climate change solutions. It explores modes of "anticipatory reconciliation," the awareness of possibilities for a less bad future already present in the current order. Unlike alienated forms of reconciliation with the present, which reproduce the status quo, anticipatory reconciliation with an unrealized yet achievable future positions consciousness against the social forces that impede a livable dystopia.

I conclude in chapter 6 with a short discussion about the meaning of hope, the fuel of dialectical thinking, in dark times. Hope is opposition to preemptive, alienated reconciliation with a social order that blocks paths to a less bad world. Today, hope is paradoxically sustained in pessimism, though a form that resists fatalism, pseudo-self-affirmation, and resignation.

Notes

1   I do not mean "increased precariousness" in the sense of a decline of long-term employment throughout the 1990s and 2000s, a thesis that is easily contested (Doogan 2001; Fevre 2007).

2   It is worth noting that Harvey (2005), drawing on Karl Polanyi, predicted that a liberal utopia, where the concept of freedom is reduced to free enterprise, can only be established through authoritarianism.

3   I am specifically referring to facial-recognition technology. There are parallel technologies that would be readily adopted, improved upon, and made accessible to all in need in a rational society, such as small, finger-mounted word-recognition cameras that convert text to speech for the blind (Hardesty 2015). Any argument against specific technologies as inherently irrational or destructive must be careful to avoid hasty generalization.

4   Sociologists may scoff at a description of a society as both alienated and anomic. The concept of alienation draws attention to social constraints on freedom while the concept of anomie draws attention to a *lack* of moral constraint, to social conditions that allow individual desires to run out of control (Horton 1964). To oversimplify, alienation is a critique of unfreedom while anomie is a critique of too much freedom. However, in the context of consumer capitalism, where alienated social forms *encourage* desires "to run wild, to ignore all limits and go on the rampage" (Bauman 2001: 16), alienation and anomie point to pathologies of the same social condition from different angles.

Chapter 2

Alienated Reconciliation: Justify, "Act," Hide

Introduction: "Humankind cannot bear very much reality"

The previous chapter summarizes our era's systemic contradictions and destructive trends that, coupled with the rapid pace of social and technological change, produce a collective unease. Perhaps due to the anthropological needs to belong to, and feel united with, a social group (see Fromm 1955), people tend to search for a sense of at-homeness in a world that feels more like a penal colony or a madhouse than a home. I term the aspiration to feel at-home with the world the goal of "reconciliation." While the term's full meaning is explicated throughout the remainder of the book, reconciliation refers to the desire to establish a sense of unity with the world, to overcome the tensions between passion and intellect, and nature and civilization. Realizing reconciliation would mean overcoming alienation (see chapter 1).

Reconciliation is unfeasible in contemporary life, though not for a lack of trying. There are numerous routes to fleetingly dull the contradiction between a desire for stability, peace, and belonging with the reality of rapid change, social contradictions, and terrifying possible futures. But there is a paradox within every effort to overcome the tension between the desire for peace and safety and the reality of change and catastrophic risks: these strategies reproduce the same conditions that produce alienation. Thus, I refer to attempts to realize reconciliation in current social conditions as modes of "alienated reconciliation," or, practices and beliefs that reconcile the individual to society in ways that maintain rather than challenge the social processes that undermine the possibility of reconciliation. Alienated reconciliation is the dimension of ideology that allows one to face the ambiguous, turbulent, and precarious world with enough assurance to fulfill one's prescribed roles and duties. Toward the future, modes of alienated reconciliation foster what William James (1961: 233) calls "the abandonment of self-responsibility" characteristic of religious experience, the sublime release of discontent by allowing "fate" to take its course without critique or resistance.

Modes of alienated reconciliation are the coping strategies of "late" capitalism. Or, as Wolfgang Streeck puts it in the introduction to *How Will Capitalism End?* (2016), *"coping, hoping, doping,* and *shopping"* are strategies individuals adopt to adapt to, and reproduce, an underregulated and disordered "post-capitalist interregnum society." One can take on the precarious and risk-packed world with self-confidence and stamina (coping), often unrealistic dreaming about the possibility of personal salvation on the horizon (hoping), using drugs to cope and enhance work performance (doping), and/or shop in the saturated markets of sweatshop-made cheap goods (shopping). All strategies must conform to a society that has left the individual out to dry without protections and a "culture of *competitive hedonism.*" Most of Streeck's typology fits under the umbrella of one general form of alienated reconciliation discussed below: *hiding.*

Modes of alienated reconciliation are temporary yet insufficient solutions to the following problems: unstable and recently extinct meaning systems, the sense that life is "out of control," worry about the future, the inability to exert sufficient control over the world to reliably bring about survival necessities, cognitive dissonance, and other forms of psychological distress. They are insufficient solutions because modes of alienated reconciliation maintain, rather than address and overcome, the social conditions that caused the latter problems. Three general forms are analyzed here:

- *Justification*: Discursive justifications[1] for the status quo. Justification reconciles the individual with reality by framing the world as right (legitimation) or fixed and unchangeable (reification) while paradoxically reproducing the social conditions that are bad enough to require justification.
- *Pseudo-activity*: Activism taken "against" the status quo that does not challenge the underlying structures that constitute current social conditions. Pseudo-activity reconciles the individual with reality by making one feel that one is doing one's part to make the world a better place while paradoxically reproducing the social conditions that motivated one to make the world less terrible.
- *Hiding*: Strategies to distract oneself or escape from the status quo. Hiding reconciles the individual with reality by producing a sense of detachment and escapism while paradoxically reproducing the social conditions that one longs to hide from.

This chapter examines contemporary manifestations of justification, pseudo-activity, and hiding. It is an analysis and critique of the techniques used to come to terms with an obviously inadequate reality, arguing that many strategies maintain the conditions that birthed the desire to come to terms with these conditions.

Because the critique of alienated reconciliation involves an analysis of lifestyles and everyday beliefs, I should make clear that my intention is not a self-righteous denunciation of the reader's way of life. Much of the critique of alienated reconciliation below is a generalization of self-critique, reflections from a life lived through alienated reconciliation, from consumerism, cynicism, vain and pointless online "debates," etc. to the implicit belief that the "action" of writing another book on social and environmental problems will help address social and environmental problems. The point of critique, as always, is to demythologize *social* life to search for possible *collective* alternatives. The very belief that one's own lifestyle is the seat of social contradictions, rather than an outcome of them, is a foundational assumption of alienated reconciliation. My goal is not to expose the hypocrisy of individuals because the fixation on exposing individual hypocrisy makes two mistaken assumptions: (1) that hypocritical individuals are the root of social problems and (2) it is possible for one to live a virtuous, unhypocritical life in present social conditions. In contrast, as argued below, the desire to live an unsoiled, honest life is partly constituted by a deeper desire to *escape* the bad social totality that undermines the possibility of living a good life.

In what follows, I first explain two conceptual bases of the notion of alienated reconciliation: Hegel's analysis of modes of "self-contained" freedom and Adorno's notion of "reconciliation under duress." Following, I explicate three general forms of alienated reconciliation—justification, pseudo-activity, and hiding—with illustrations. Unlike Hegel's account of modes of self-contained freedom, explained shortly, the three general modes of alienated reconciliation are not meant to be read as the movement and evolution of consciousness from lower to higher states. While alienated reconciliation can begin with justification ("It's not so bad"), drift into pseudo-activity ("OK, this is bad. What can *I* do to help?"), and culminate in hiding ("The world can't be saved so I may as well meditate"), consciousness may tour daily through all three modes or take up permanent residence in one modality for a lifetime.

Conceptual background

Fortified by the ideas of Mark Fisher, Slavoj Žižek, and other contemporary theorists, two older lines of thought inform the notion of alienated reconciliation: Hegel's analysis of the futility of purely cognitive and individualist paths to freedom in his *Phenomenology* and Adorno's consistent protest against "false reconciliation" with reality, especially through the practice of "pseudo-activity." I discuss both in turn.

Hegel on slave ideology

The chapter on self-consciousness in Hegel's *Phenomenology* is an account of the subject's inability to eliminate objective preconditions for the self and freedom, whereby we "learn that a certain sort of objectivity is essential to being a subject" (Krasnoff 2008: 94). It is an examination of the practical human self, action, and agency in social context—specifically, hierarchical relations between master and slave—and a critique of individualist, asociological understandings of freedom and agency. The point is to reveal that the self and freedom are in part dependent on external social conditions.

Following the famous section on the master-slave dialectic, where consciousness comes to terms with the historical contingency of authoritative social norms, Hegel examines forms of self-consciousness that unsuccessfully pursue freedom by deceptively declaring independence from external constraints: stoicism, ancient skepticism, and the "unhappy consciousness," a term Hegel uses to describe medieval Christian consciousness as well as related forms of thought in the pre-Christian Greek world (Pinkard 1994: 70). Each phase leads to self-deception, forms of "partial self-liberation" that act as "substitutes" for real freedom (Lauer 1993: 135). Alexandre Kojève (1969) interprets Hegel's analysis as a critique of the ideologies the slave dreams up to reconcile his reality of bondage with the ideal of freedom because all represent futile attempts to attain freedom and distract the slave from what must actually take place to attain freedom: fight the master and end their hierarchical relationship.

Following the slave's awareness of the social contingency of norms, stoicism interprets freedom as "freedom in *thinking*" (Pinkard 1994: 63). This is an incoherent and unsatisfactory freedom because it is merely an abstracted idea of freedom, completely formal without content, and a byproduct of a society of competition, fear, and servitude (Marcuse 1960: 119). Stoicism is self-contradictory because, among other reasons, the external world is still a determinant of a supposedly "free" thought and its lifeless formalism is simply too tedious and boring for an active being like humanity (Kojève 1969: 54; Lauer 1993: 138; Pinkard 1994: 66f). In short, the stoic is reduced to talking about rather than realizing freedom, which is *wearisome* (Hegel 1967: 246).

The skeptic addresses the limitations of stoicism by generalizing the stoic claim of independence by "rejecting the standards and values he finds in his everyday life" (Krasnoff 2008: 107). Kojève (1969: 54) describes skepticism as nihilistic and solipsistic, where the value and reality of the world is negated. The skeptic's view is also self-contradictory and therefore unsatisfactory: his own existence contradicts the premise of the non-value and/or non-reality of the world and his supposed freedom is established by affirming his impersonal, detached perspective yet knowing, as a skeptic, that his own view is merely subjective. Further, his identity as a skeptic depends on the very world he claims to negate. Hegel (1967: 250) says the skeptic is aware of his contradictory perspective, yet the two sides of his internal contradictory conversation are like "self-willed children" who "procure the joy of remaining in contradiction."

To overcome the contradictions of skepticism, a new ideology emerges whereby he acknowledges his existence as a slave but justifies his bondage by producing a vision of two worlds that first emerged in skepticism: the empirical, finite world, where every being is in chains, and a Beyond, where the ideal of freedom reigns (Kojève 1969: 55). Hegel calls this the "unhappy consciousness" that characterizes the tragic Christian longing for a qualitatively different, transcendent world that cannot be realized. This form of self-consciousness is attained when the skeptic "owns up to the idea that there are certain things that he claims to know and certain values that he accepts that he cannot willingly change nor would want to change; he simply admits that he has no way of justifying those beliefs outside of his contingently held point of view" (Pinkard 1994: 69). The unhappy consciousness holds worldly, subjective norms and values but knows they lack a now-unattainable universal justification.

Whereas Hegel's analysis uncovers unsatisfactory and inconsistent attitudes and perspectives through which one tries to "retrieve independence in a frustrating world" (Cohen 1994: 162), to overcome the contradiction between the ideal of freedom and the reality of bondage, this chapter is an analysis of strategies through which people strive to transcend the contradiction between a desire for stability and peace and the reality of being "doomed on all fronts" in a rapidly changing world (see chapter 1). The analysis is intimately linked to Hegel because it assumes, like Hegel, that humans crave "absolute stability and constancy amid change and uncertainty" and seek to overcome the "mental chaos" felt in periods of rapid social change, such as the end of the Roman Empire (Baillie 1967: 241). Further, like Hegel and, later, Marx, I also assume that overcoming contradictions, whether between the ideal of freedom and the reality of bondage or between the desire for peace and the reality of social disorder, is, or will be, a *social* achievement. This assumption becomes clearer in the second half of the book.

Adorno on "reconciliation under duress"
Along with Hegel's account of the limits of self-contained freedom,

this chapter builds on Adorno's analyses of self-defeating and deceptive attempts to overcome social contradictions. He has a penchant for exposing contradictions that cannot be solved within existing society and explaining why strategies to transcend contradictions in existing conditions are necessarily unsatisfactory, illusionary, and even destructive. The closest Adorno (1977) comes to covering this line of argument under a single concept is in the title of his case against Lukács' critique of modernist art, "*Erpresste Versöhnung*": "reconciliation under duress" or "extorted reconciliation." In the case of aesthetics, Adorno's point is that art expressing the real alienation of the present condition (e.g., Schoenberg's atonal music) is more enlightening than art masking real alienation (e.g., socialist realism) (Jay 1984: 255). Others have adopted similar terms to describe Adorno's argument in its many instances, including "preemptive" or "premature" reconciliation (Harrington 2001; Gordon 2016) as well as "false" and "coerced" reconciliation (Jarvis 1998). Because these pseudo-remedies are attempts to reconcile the damaged individual with the social conditions that produce alienation, I think the term "alienated reconciliation" is especially helpful and evocative, a paradox best illustrated by Adorno's conversation with Hegel and his notion of "pseudo-activity."

Given the discussion of Hegel above, a helpful way to introduce Adorno's argument is his critique of Hegelian philosophy's own false reconciliation with reality. Adorno is suspicious of "the positive dialectics found in Hegel, where philosophy marches forward in the world through resolving the contradictions of human history and experience" (Bayoumi 2005: 52), a belief clearest in his theory of the state and history (Hegel 1956, 1976), a conformist logic already present in the *Phenomenology* (Marcuse 1960). According to Adorno, Hegel promotes false reconciliation because he believes that "the modern state and history have come about as necessary conclusions in a logical development" and individuals "must approve of and identify with the state and history" (Baumann 2011: 86). As Gordon (2016: 185) put it:

> a major distinction between nineteenth-century Hegelian dialectics and the late modern mode of dialectical reasoning known as critical theory was that the latter resisted Hegel's original ideal of a thoroughgoing reconciliation between subject and object, universal and particular. Against the dialectical overcoming of difference as theorized by Hegel, Adorno believed that under present-day conditions of totalizing social domination, in which the subject's freedom threatened to vanish entirely, critical theory was charged with the task of sustaining difference and negativity rather than seeking their premature reconciliation.

Although Adorno's positive conception of reconciliation, discussed in chapter 4, is influenced by Hegel's notion of a "concrete universal" as "unity in difference" (Baumann 2011: 80), he believes that reconciliation is a goal to be aimed for, to be realized through social change, rather than an already actual condition or, importantly, one that necessarily emerges through teleological historical progress (see chapter 3).

Adorno's notion of "pseudo-activity" as a form of renunciation serves as another illustration of reconciliation under duress. In one of his last essays, "Resignation" (1991), Adorno responds to the common criticism of the Frankfurt School's pessimism as too impractical and quietist to be of any use to radicals who want to change the world. He makes the case that one can be falsely reconciled to the status quo by ostensibly "taking action" against the status quo. Those who distrust intellectuals who do not "get their hands dirty" or fail to provide an immediate plan for action are, according to Adorno, responding to bad news out of fear and anger, which is misdirected at the bearer of bad news rather than the bad news itself. The "prohibition of thinking" implied in the demand to *Get out there and actually do something* sprouts from a repressed knowledge of a lack of a revolutionary situation: "[o]ne clings to action because of the impossibility of action" (Adorno 1991: 172).

The only activism permitted today is "pseudo-activity," a form of action that "overplays itself and fires itself up for the sake of its own publicity without admitting to what degree it serves as a substitute for satisfaction, thus elevating itself to an end in itself" (Adorno 1991: 173). Pseudo-activity is a "substitute for satisfaction" for "those behind bars" who desire freedom. To put Adorno's point in conversation with Hegel's chapter on self-consciousness, the slave trades in his "autonomous thinking" for a "new security" in pseudo-activity, springing to action precisely because he knows he cannot free himself in current social conditions. For now, Adorno says, it would be better to retain his limited freedom of thought, so he is able to overcome the master-slave relation when or if the real possibility for change beckons (see chapter 5).

This chapter focuses on the way alienated reconciliation manifests itself today in response to the contradictions discussed in chapter 1. Three general modes of alienated reconciliation are identified: justification, pseudo-activity, and hiding.

Justify

Justification refers to both of the prominent lines of thought through which ideology rationalizes the status quo and dismisses the reality of social contradictions: (1) the current social formation is right, or could be made right with minor adjustments (*legitimation*), and (2) the status quo is the way it is and cannot be different (*reification*). Legitimation spans lofty, systematic philosophies of justice employed to defend the current order to everyday statements that rationalize what happens to already exist. Legitimation here includes any normative justification for the most basic structural conditions of society (e.g., the private ownership of the means of production). Thus, it is possible, for example, to criticize high levels of inequality on normative grounds while simultaneously legitimating the structural conditions that produced high levels of inequality.

Reification does not justify the status quo through an appeal to ideals and norms, but, instead, by constituting the social order as fixed and unchangeable. Reification, a more potent form of justification in a society that rarely believes in its own legitimations, has pre-cognitive origins in the "undiscussed," unquestioned, merely-lived social world (Bourdieu 1977: 164ff) and its routine practices (Althusser 1971) that seem *natural* due to their taken-for-grantedness, yet are, in reality, historically formed and contingent (Gunderson 2020). However, due to historical forgetfulness, this pre-cognitive level of reification transforms into reificatory discursive forms, from everyday naturalizations of the social world (e.g., "This is just the way things are") to the theoretical consciousness of some strains of social sciences that essentialize and naturalize the historical and contingent (e.g., the "crude materialism" of economists; see Marx 1973: 687; cf. Berger and Pullberg 1965: 207).

This section analyzes two prominent discursive forms of justification today: "utopian pragmatism" and "neoliberal naturalism." Utopian pragmatism is an appeal to centrist and "moderate" political frameworks that emphasize "realistic" and "workable" solutions to the massive global problems discussed in chapter 1. Neoliberal naturalism is a common contemporary form of reification that strives to naturalize contingent social processes, some of which have only existed for 4 or 5 decades.

Both utopian pragmatism and neoliberal naturalism are two heads of a more foundational and usually unreflected assumption that there is no alternative to capitalism, a "pervasive atmosphere" that acts "as a kind of invisible barrier constraining thought and action" that Fisher (2009: 16) terms "capitalist realism." In other words, utopian pragmatism and neoliberal naturalism are the primary manifestations of legitimation and reification, respectively, that discursively reinforce the "widespread sense that not only is capitalism the only viable political and economic system, but also that it is now impossible even to *imagine* a coherent alternative to it" (Fisher 2009: 2).

Utopian pragmatism

Marx, an "anti-utopian utopian" (Jacoby 2005), is critical of two kinds of "starry-eyed idealist" utopianisms (Eagleton 2016). The first is the blueprint thinking of the utopian socialists like Fourier who tried to detail the fine points of an ideal society, down to the ideal schedule of an ideal day. The other idealist utopians are of the seemingly opposite persuasion: the matter-of-fact "realists," who are, in fact:

> wild-eyed idealists who hold that the future will be pretty much like the present. Those with their heads truly in the clouds are the hard-headed pragmatists who seem to assume that Mars bars and the International Monetary Fund will still be with us in 500 years' time. Our system is run by a set of dreamers who call themselves realists. (Eagleton 2016: 416)

This is precisely what is meant by *utopian pragmatism,* which is "pragmatic" due to an emphasis on solutions that work within the status quo (usually termed "realistic," "pragmatic," "achievable," "workable," or "cautious" solutions) yet "utopian" in the very belief that the status quo can be sustained (cf. Žižek 2007).

Utopian pragmatism is the taken-for-granted, common-sensical ideology undergirding contemporary political discourse, despite its self-understanding as the end of ideology. It is the fantasy that liberal capitalism is the "end of history," the vast ocean of unquestioned common ground between center-left and center-right political parties, grave grumblings against "ideological purity" with pleas to vote for corporate-friendly ("moderate") representatives, and the conviction that even social democracy is too radical for the current era. Utopian pragmatism manifests in many forms, from worrying more about the "end of civility" than the widening wealth inequality and resentment that fuels the end of civility, to the deification of former president Barack Obama—who bailed out the institutions that caused the 2008 financial crisis, oversaw the forcible deportation of over 3 million undocumented immigrants, and directed the massive upscaling of a civil rights-abusing domestic surveillance program and international law-violating drone program—and the resurrectory embrace of former president George W. Bush, whose central war led to around a half million deaths (Hagopian et al. 2013) and the rise of ISIS.

As capitalist realism in the form of legitimation, what all utopian pragmatisms have in common is the usually unstated assumption that opposition to capitalism is utopian and unrealistic while an affirmation of capitalism is realistic. However, the affirmation of capitalism is typically passive and indirect. Few can say capitalism is great with a straight face. Instead, the bad is justified through contrast with the very bad: projects that strive to qualitatively change the status quo, which will, according to the post-ideology ideology of capitalist realism, inevitably lead to fanaticism and totalitarianism (Fisher 2009).

We live in a contradiction: a brutal state of affairs, profoundly inegalitarian – where all existence is evaluated in terms of money alone – is presented to us as ideal. To justify their conservatism, the partisans of the established order cannot really call it ideal or wonderful. So instead, they have decided to say that all the rest is horrible. Sure, they say, we may not live in a condition of perfect Goodness. But we're lucky that we don't live in a condition of Evil. Our democracy is not perfect. But it's better than the bloody dictatorships. Capitalism is unjust. But it's not criminal like Stalinism. We let millions of Africans die of AIDS, but we don't make racist nationalist declarations like Milosevic. We kill Iraqis with our airplanes, but we don't cut their throats with machetes like they do in Rwanda, etc. (Badiou in Cox and Whalen 2001: 69)

From this usually implicit and unquestioned starting point, the utopian pragmatist believes that the only alternative to capitalism as it is today is capitalism with minor modifications. Utopian pragmatism views anti-capitalism as a radical, unrealistic position, yet "supporting capitalism, an ideology that is changing the biophysical conditions that defined the Holocene and is threatening life on Earth, is considered a moderate decision" (Prádanos 2018: 12).

Herein lies utopian pragmatism's most radically utopian assumption: the basic workings of the current social order, which threaten our species' long-term survival, can persist into the long-term future with minor modifications (cf. Fisher 2008: 18). As discussed in chapter 1, there is a systemic contradiction between capital's needs to expand and the destructive impacts that capitalist growth has on an especially important "condition of production": the climate system. Despite this paradox, capitalist processes are continually sold as the solution to the environmental harms caused by capitalist processes. The case for "green growth" is a clear illustration of this contradiction of utopian pragmatism.

Green growth is a policy framework that imagines that there are multiple "synergies" between economic growth and environmental protection through green stimulus packages, market-correction policies, and green industrial innovation (i.e., a technological transformation that leads to improvements in efficiency and increased reliance on renewable energy sources) (Jacobs 2013). The idea that the economy can benefit from environmental protection is wildly popular in corporate and policy spheres (e.g., Organization for Economic Co-operation and Development [OECD] 2011; World Bank 2012). Yet there is a problem with widespread faith in green growth: economic growth is one of the major drivers of carbon emissions (York et al. 2003; Stern 2006; Jorgenson & Clark 2012; Burke et al. 2015) and it is highly unlikely that an absolute decoupling of carbon emissions from economic growth is possible, especially at the rate necessary to avoid catastrophic warming: "[w]hile we find some reduction in the linkage between economic growth and territorial emissions, once we account for high-income countries' offshoring of emissions, there is no evidence of decoupling" (Knight and Schor 2014: 3729; for summaries, see Hickel 2019; Hickel and Kallis 2019; Schor and Jorgenson 2019). In fact, according to climate scientists Anderson and Bows (2011, 2012), a *reduction* in growth in overdeveloped countries is necessary to stay within climate targets.

In addition to fictionalizing the relationship between growth and emissions, the central mechanisms of the impossible goal of green growth have failed to substantially reduce carbon emissions. Carbon markets have had negligible impacts (Muûls et al. 2016) and efficiency improvements are an insufficient route to tackle climate change given that total emissions have *increased* despite increases in global carbon efficiency (York 2010) and efficiency improvements at a national level are associated with *higher* CO_2 emissions, electricity consumption, and energy use (York and McGee 2016). The more pernicious implication of utopian pragmatism is social reproduction and a derailing of radical solutions. For example, Lohmann (2005) shows how the Kyoto Protocol's emphasis on carbon markets, an approach proposed by the US, who later failed to ratify the treaty, redirected intellectual and financial resources from alternative policies and social changes that have the potential to actually significantly reduce emissions. Criticisms of the Protocol in favor of stronger mitigation policies were then scorned as a "do-nothing" stance.

Utopian pragmatism reconciles consciousness to reality with the promise that all will be well if we stay on course. It does not rise to the level of pseudo-activity because it does not require action from the individual. In fact, due to its dream that the status quo can be made sustainable, utopian pragmatism reduces the likelihood of action (cf. Stuart et al. 2020b). It is an alienated form of reconciliation precisely because of its belief that capitalism can be made sustainable. The paradoxical consolation of utopian pragmatism is this: the system may be cooking the planet, but alternatives are unrealistic.

Neoliberal naturalism

Neoliberal naturalism refers to the naturalization of the historically contingent social condition associated with financial deregulation, an emphasis on individualism, "flexible" labor, austerity, privatization, a state wholly submissive to business interests, and widening inequality. I will focus on the latter consequence of neoliberalism here. Rather than explaining "the slew of privatizations that took place since the 1980s," which, not long ago, were believed to be the unrealizable utopian dreams of a small group of economists (Fisher 2009: 17), neoliberal naturalism takes their consequences as taken-for-granted fact and then retroactively "explains"—really, describes—what emerged with biological metaphors. This section provides a quintessential example of neoliberal naturalism, makes the case that neoliberal naturalism should be analytically distrusted because it cannot explain variation across societies, and concludes with a reflection on the comforts of achieving alienated reconciliation via reification. I focus on the empirical arguments of neoliberal naturalism before analyzing the reconciliation it provides because the comforts of neoliberal naturalism are, like all subjective reifications, built into its mythological constitution of changeable social facts as unchangeable natural facts.

Before continuing, it is worth clarifying that I think evolutionary theory should inform theories of human behavior. However, evolutionary theory is better suited to do so if it does *not* assume that "natural selection acting on genes will produce behavior and social structures that optimize genetic reproductive fitness" for a number of reasons, the most notable being that sociocultural change does not necessarily maximize genetic fitness (Dietz et al. 1990: 158; for readable discussions, see Richerson and Boyd 2005; York and Mancus 2009).[2] However, it is very unlikely that I will change the reader's beliefs about the "nature versus nurture" question—which is not a "versus" question at all—in a short section, so I will not try. Instead, my first goal is to convince the reader that, even if there is a biological foundation for social life, which is true, biological-determinist frameworks cannot explain the vast variability in human behavior and social forms across cultures and over time.

The inability of biological-determinist theories of stratification to explain historical variation in inequality is especially apparent in the case of neoliberal naturalism. Unlike traditional social Darwinism, which, for all its faults, was sophisticated enough to try to naturalize capitalism as an evolutionary *social* form that *emerged* from past social forms (Spencer 1921: Part 5), what is remarkable about neoliberal naturalism is its effort to naturalize the consequences of a roughly half-century old social form, without any attempt to explain its emergence. Take a popular case of neoliberal naturalism from Canadian psychologist and public intellectual Jordan Peterson's best-selling *12 Rules for Life* (2018), a self-help book with recipes to achieve alienated reconciliation, which he calls "antidotes to chaos." Peterson analogizes the physiological and ecological bases for the establishment of hierarchies between lobsters in conflict over resources to human hierarchies. After summarizing research on the "dispute resolutions" of lobsters, from flight to fight, and the differences in serotonin and octopamine levels in dominant and subordinate lobsters, he states:

> [w]hen a defeated lobster regains its courage and dares to fight again it is more likely to lose again than you would predict, statistically, from a tally of its previous fights. Its victorious opponent, on the other hand, is more likely to win. It's winner-take-all in the lobster world, just as it is in human societies, where the top 1 percent have as much loot as the bottom 50 percent—and where the richest eighty-five people have as much money as the bottom three and a half billion. (Peterson 2018: 8)

He goes on to apply this "basic principle" of unequal distribution to the dominance of a few composers in classical music in orchestras, the popularity of a few authors in book sales, and other areas. I will focus on the explanation for income and wealth inequality here (for an extensive leftist critique of Peterson's work, see Burgis et al. 2020).

If we are to take an account of social inequality seriously, it should be able to explain, or at least propose explanations for, perennial questions in stratification research: Why are some societies more unequal than others? What causes stratification patterns to change over time? In contrast, Peterson points to a couple of isolated facts about social stratification patterns that happen to exist now, and purports to explain them with a basic principle of unequal distribution. However, a general principle of unequal distribution cannot *explain* stratification patterns across human history, a species that have lived in relatively egalitarian societies for the vast majority of their history (Kerbo 2012). But one does not need to enter "prehistory" for counterfactuals.

For example, levels of wealth inequality have skyrocketed in the past half century (Inequality.org 2020), a minuscule amount of time from an evolutionary perspective. Perhaps neoliberal naturalists could piece together an explanation based on alleged changes in brain chemistry, or other natural changes resulting from accelerated lobster-like battles between subordinates and superordinates; between those "defeated-looking, scrunched-up, inhibited, drooping, skulking sort of lobster[s], very likely to hang around street corners, and to vanish at the first hint of trouble" (Peterson 2018: 7), and those who know the first Rule of Life: "Stand up straight with your shoulders back." But then one would have to also explain why inequality remains relatively low in, for example, Northern European social-democratic countries (World Inequality Lab 2018), why levels of social mobility are *higher* in countries with *less* social inequality (Corak 2013), and other correlations that make little sense from a neoliberal-naturalistic perspective.

Yet I suspect that these elemental historical-comparative questions that should be addressed in any viable theory of social stratification do not concern neoliberal naturalists because explaining human behavior is a subordinate aim. Like any intellectual form of reification, explanation is secondary to, and derivative of, naturalization, i.e., constituting the contingent as fixed and the historically formed as unchangeable. For example, take the following leap in Peterson's (2018: 4) discussion of hierarchies in chickens and songbirds:

[i]f a contagious avian disease sweeps through a neighbourhood of well-stratified songbirds, it is the least dominant and most stressed birds, occupying the lowest rungs of the bird world, who are most likely to sicken and die. This is equally true of human neighbourhoods, when bird flu viruses and other illnesses sweep across the planet. The poor and stressed always die first, and in greater numbers. They

are also much more susceptible to non-infectious diseases, such as cancer, diabetes and heart disease.

What is misleading is the inference that what is true of birds of the "lowest rungs of the bird world" is "equally true" of "poor and stressed" humans. This is misleading because human poverty rates and resultant health outcomes are not naturally determined, fixed, unchangeable facts, but, instead, what Durkheim (1938) famously calls *social* facts: human created, supraindividual forces that exert an external power over individuals. Again, one only needs comparative-historical analysis to see that poverty and unequal health outcomes are social rather than natural facts. For example, more egalitarian countries are healthier (Wilkinson and Pickett 2011). Further, avian flus and other diseases are now incubated and accelerated in factory farms, a relatively recent—not transhistorical—form of animal agriculture that uses industrial technologies and close confinement for the historically particular purpose—not a "natural," let alone historically typical, purpose—of maximizing profits (Hollenbeck 2016).

Neoliberal naturalists may reply, "I too think poor people dying of preventable diseases is sad. But things are the way they are. Facts don't care about your feelings." And they will no doubt suspect that this analysis of their explanatory framework as ideology is rooted in soft-mindedness and weakness, an unwillingness to accept a harsh reality. What is implied in both replies, however, is that the current social order is fixed and unchangeable. It is not. What is often construed as a tough-minded if tragic perspective is actually one of intellectual frailty: one cannot face the fact that the lion's share of contemporary suffering results from *contingent* yet law-like social structures that emerged through an arbitrary and still blind process of human history. Peterson (2018: xxv) and the existentialists before him may be right that there is a "suffering that is intrinsic to Being,"[3] but such abstractions say nothing about why, for example, a quarter of people aged 18 to 64 who live in the richest society to ever exist have trouble paying medical bills, and that a fifth of Americans with medical bill problems declare bankruptcy (Hamel et al. 2016). It is much easier to look away from socially-produced suffering and repeat the consoling myth, "This is just the way things are" (cf. Gunderson 2020). In contrast, real tough-mindedness is resolute attention to the *social* causes of the current order and potential alternatives. Genuine tragic insight is knowing that alternatives exist yet are left unrealized, and holding this impasse in consciousness without cowering to a mythology dressed up as science.

"Act"

When justification fails to smooth over systemic contradictions with fairy tales, and the resulting cognitive dissonance renders passive alienated reconciliation impossible, one may pursue an active form of alienated reconciliation: getting involved in activism that reproduces, rather than changes, the world that can no longer be justified.

Adorno (1991) remarks that a "do-it-yourself" mentality underlies pseudo-activity. It is "rationalized through the acceptance of any small change as one step on the long way toward total change," especially faith in the activism of small groups (Adorno 1991. 173). Pseudo-activity usually flows from the following reasoning: "since attempts at big systemic change have failed, all we can do is act small," a belief critiqued by Klein (2019: 131) in the context of climate politics. "Small" includes individual lifestyle changes, simple acts of charity, a life devoted to "do-gooding," and a focus on local solutions.

Not only are the methods of pseudo-activists ineffective, but the acts themselves encourage passivity because they reconcile the activist to the society they are trying to change by, for example, sparing the activist of "the cognition of his impotence" (Adorno 1991: 174). That feeling of having "done something" alone or perhaps with a group is withdrawal from reality. I focus on two prominent manifestations of pseudo-activity: *moralizing individualism* and *do-gooding*.

Moralizing individualism

Moralizing individualism refers to the individualization and culturalization of the causes of structural problems, and the tendency to only moralize against, as opposed to analyze, explain, and discuss, these problems. Structural explanations are replaced with individual and cultural explanations, and moralizing performs as a substitute for thought. As is well-known, these strategies have long been essential to conservatism, where poverty, for example, is framed as a byproduct of individual laziness and a culture of poverty. What is more notable is that moralizing individualism is now common among identitarian liberals (sometimes termed "cultural leftists"). This section summarizes Fisher's (2013) case against moralizing individualism, explains the real-world implications of moralizing individualism through an analysis of the fat acceptance movement, and explains why moralizing individualism is a form of alienated reconciliation.

Written in response to the "finger-wagging sermon[s]" and "kangaroo courts" of the humorless "leftists" of Twitter who "call out" and lecture other users, typically other leftists, about their "problematic" views and behaviors, Fisher's (2013) "Exiting the Vampire Castle" is one of the finest critiques of this manifestation of pseudo-activity, where the term "moralizing individualism" is taken. His objections to moralizing individualism masquerading as leftist politics are many, but there is a unifying argument that such a pseudo-politics undercuts solidarity, the ability to locate the structural causes of social problems, and the possibility of a unified movement to change the social order due to its penchant for identitarianism and individualizing blame. I discuss each tendency in turn.

First, moralizing individualism almost always ignores questions of class in favor of identity. Class politics becomes a side affair and is usually snobbishly snubbed before it can even come to the surface: "the sheer mention of class is now automatically treated as if that means one is trying to downgrade the importance of race and gender" (Fisher 2013). This "Vampire's Castle" of identity politics is a market of "academic capital" where identitarian liberals cash in their marginalized identities, or their heroic online actions as "allies," for increased academic status. Liberal identitarianism undermines working-class solidarity by, for example, trying to convince black workers that they share similar material interests with Obama or Kamala Harris and misdiagnosing, and thereby perpetuating, the causes of the very real problems of racism, sexism, transphobia, etc. (e.g., Michaels 2010; Reed 2018a). To provide only one example, the post-structuralist "radicals" Judith Butler and Donna Haraway financially contributed to the presidential campaign of Harris (Featherstone 2019)—who supported exceptionally punitive policies as San Francisco's district attorney and California's attorney general (Marcetic 2017; Bragman and Colangelo 2019)—despite her running against an actually progressive alternative (Sanders). The point here is not to shame these two individuals, which would accomplish nothing, but to offer a small illustration of how, as Marxists have long warned, prioritizing culture and identity undermines class politics and the possibility of rebuilding a socialist movement (see also Reed 2018b).

A second way that moralizing individualism undermines solidarity and obscures the structural causes of systemic contradictions is individualizing blame through guilt and essentialism. According to Fisher, we have allowed the so-called left to become an arena "where class has disappeared, but moralism is everywhere, where solidarity is impossible, but guilt and fear are omnipresent." More perniciously, it individualizes blame by essentializing the given "problematic" behavior: one who makes a crude remark that may be sexist, racist, etc., or could be construed as such, then *becomes* a sexist, racist, etc. based on that remark. Character assassinations following a minor faux pas or more serious unethical behavior leaves the "stench of bad conscience and witch-hunting moralism." How does one build a movement to transform the social order while simultaneously supporting a candidate who calls potential comrades a "basket of deplorables"?

The great paradox of moralizing individualism from identitarian liberals is that it strengthens its enemies like the cultural right. For example, the Trump presidency was partly a vote *against* the Democratic Party's "progressive neoliberalism"— "an alliance of mainstream currents of new social movements (feminism, anti-racism, multiculturalism, and LGBTQ rights), on the one side, and high-end 'symbolic' and service-based business sectors (Wall Street, Silicon Valley, and Hollywood), on the other" (Fraser 2017). Further, the massive popularity of Jordan Peterson was built on his ability to address "what many of us feel goes wrong in the PC universe of obsessive regulation" (Žižek 2018) and the online "activism" of identitarian liberals helped fuel, though did not independently cause, the rise of the alt-right (Nagle 2017). To be clear, the resurgence of the far right is first and foremost a reactionary response to the systemic contradictions described in chapter 1. However, this violent, thrashing reaction repeatedly and swiftly memeifies the moralizing-individualist exclamations of identarian liberals as fodder to grow its ranks.

While the "active" aspect of moralizing individualism as pseudo-activity typically manifests as carefully drafting Twitter posts, the culturalist-individualist-moralist framework has real implications that reproduce the status quo, or even make it worse. The "fat acceptance movement" is a clear illustration.

The approach of the "class left" to the obesity epidemic is to identify the structural drivers of the epidemic in order to address them. For example, obesity rates are higher among those with low incomes and low education levels (Sobal and Stunkard 1989; Molarius et al. 2000), in part because "the way to get the most calories for the least money is to eat a diet that is high in fat and sugar" (Mitchell et al. 2011: 2; see Drewnowski and Specter 2004; Wyatt et al. 2006: 173). From here, one proposes and organizes support for poverty-reduction policies coupled with programs that make healthy food affordable and accessible, such as heavily subsidizing organic vegetables and fruit production and urban agriculture programs as well as ending subsidies for unhealthy agricultural and food sectors.

In contrast, the approach of the fat acceptance movement is, according to a co-chair of the National Association to Advance Fat Acceptance, a cultural fight against "size discrimination" and "fat stigma" (White in Sheehan 2010). On the one hand, everyone should support "fat acceptance" in the sense of opposing size-based discrimination in employment, healthcare, and other arenas and reject individualized explanations for obesity rates (Forse and Krishnamurty 2015). Further, not all causes of obesity are controllable as there are genetic predispositions increasing the likelihood of being overweight and obese (for summary, see Wyatt et al. 2006: 172). However, because environmental causes are historical and changeable, they ought to be changed due to the serious health consequences of obesity, including heart disease, diabetes, certain cancers, and death (Wyatt et al. 2006). Instead, the fat acceptance movement leaves untouched the structural causes of obesity and associated negative health outcomes through such measures as fighting against the "negative" and "prejudiced" word "obese," inspiring fashion designers to be cognizant of plus-sized consumers, and opposition to "making changes to one's body at the request of another person" (i.e., reduce the pressure to lose weight) (White in Sheehan 2010).

Such a political practice demands that culture adapts to the reality of increasing obesity rates, which is accepted as a given, and stigmatizes the "fat stigma" of those who argue that increasing obesity rates are a real health problem rather than a problem of identity misinterpretation.

Moralizing individualism is reconciliatory because, like any moralism, it gives the sermonizer the self-impression that they are on the right side of history, a "knight of virtue," to misapply Hegel's (1967: 406) quip, battling a debased world, usually through social media, by "changing the conversation," which typically means depantsing fellow internet-addicts in the virtual sanatorium's community room. It is an alienated form of reconciliation because, by focusing on culture and identity, it reproduces or even accelerates the structural conditions that cause alienation. By individualizing blame, it actively reduces the probability of an organized social movement that could change the social order.

Do-gooding

While moralizing individualism refers to a moralistic approach to "politics" that attempts to achieve cultural change by making individuals with "problematic" beliefs and practices feel guilty, do-gooding refers to attempts to improve social conditions through other forms of individual activism, typically forms that require looking away from a phone or computer screen. Here, I am implicitly contrasting *individual* activism, where one tries to change the world alone or in small groups outside of traditional political arenas, with *collective-political* activism, or building broad-based political movements that strive to transform existing social structures by taking or toppling state power. (I would exclude purely expressive social movements from collective-*political* activism. Movements that do not intend to alter social conditions through politics—taking power, instituting policy, etc.—are instances of pseudo-activity for the same reason as individual activism. A "movement" that exclusively consists of expressive protests has the same structure of individual activism, despite the performances being executed in close proximity to others. Both are forms of social reproduction that permit the activist to *feel* as though they are challenging the social order despite reproducing it.)

Individual activism includes everything from small charitable contributions to making innumerable personal sacrifices to do as much good as possible through individual action. As Larissa MacFarquhar explains in *Strangers Drowning* (2015), which analyzes many cases of these latter extreme do-gooders, it is tempting and easy to be critical of do-gooders for the wrong reasons. Because they hold up a mirror that shows how much more we can and should do, a critique of do-gooders may often grow from a rationalization of our own failure to live a better life. The analysis of do-gooding below is not a dismissal of those who try to be decent people or, as a more realistic goal, to live "less wrongly" (Freyenhagen 2013), but, instead, a critique of the belief that collective problems can be solved through individual action. Further, my goal is not to explore the old questions of whether altruism can ever be truly selfless, or if it is really virtuous. Instead, the goal of this section is to examine how a noble aim such as do-gooding actualizes as alienated reconciliation.

Do-gooding often springs from helplessness felt at the sight of global injustices that are out of one's control. In the face of the scale of systemic contradictions discussed in chapter 1, one asks, "What can I do?" The obvious if painful answer in an absence of a political infrastructure to address these issues is, "Very little." Escaping the dissonance of "Very little" is the soil in which much do-gooding grows. Do-gooding is an advanced form of reconciliation with a contradictory reality because it is the only route through which one can escape from the dissonance of the individual's hope to change the world despite the reality of the individual's powerlessness to do so. However, it is an alienated form of reconciliation because individual activism really is powerless to change the conditions that produce alienation: "[t]he problem is that the model of individual responsibility assumed by most versions of ethics have little purchase on the behavior of Capital or corporations" (Fisher 2008: 66-67). Ethical consumerism, billionaire philanthropy, and the intentional decision to be childfree all illustrate this contradiction.

Ethical consumerism is do-gooding built on the premise that you can "vote with your dollar" (Shaw et al. 2006). By providing economic incentives or disincentives for producers, the argument goes, consumer decisions can lead to progressive social changes, such as improving working conditions and environmental health. The reconciliatory feeling produced by ethical consumerism is described well by Žižek (2011: 117) in the context of purchasing a fairly traded cup of coffee:

[w]hen ... confronted with the starving child, we are told: "For the price of a couple of cappuccinos, you can continue in your ignorant and pleasurable life, not only not feeling any guilt, but even feeling good for having participated in the struggle against suffering!"

Despite this "feel good" factor produced by ethical consumerism, well-known and exploited by marketers, the track record of corporations following through on their social and ecological promises to ethical shoppers is slim. For example, based on a random sample of publicly listed companies in food, textile, and wood-products sectors, Thorlakson et al. (2018) show that companies who use at least one form of "sustainable sourcing practice" (52 percent) (e.g., third-party organic certification) typically only address one or a few inputs (71 percent) and rarely address environmental issues. In addition to being ineffective, corporate entities such as Whole Foods Market have individualized and depoliticized the solutions to social and ecological problems, thereby undermining the collective-political solutions (Johnston 2008). Similarly, Guthman (2007: 264) argues "food politics has become a progenitor of a neoliberal anti-politics that devolves regulatory responsibility to consumers via their dietary choices." Like other forms of pseudo-activity, ethical consumerism reproduces the status quo while making actors feel as though they are toppling it (Gunderson 2014).

The hidden contradictions of do-gooding are more obvious when the do-gooding is performed by the corporate and ruling classes. Anand Giridharadas' *Winners Take All* (2018) shows how charitable campaigns of philanthropic billionaires, and their privatized plans to save the world, are processes of social reproduction rather than humanitarian-led social transformations. The ostensibly humanitarian corporate class lobbies for policies that vacuum wealth upwards and contributes to the widening of social inequality while simultaneously marketing themselves as do-gooders for running "socially responsible" businesses, participating in "impact investing," and pursuing other initiatives that keep intact the system that benefits the philanthropist and harms his alleged object of concern. There is not just a hypocrisy in the "milking—and perhaps abetting—of an unjust status quo and the attempts by the milkers to repair a small part of it" (Giridharadas 2018. 7), there is, more importantly, a structural *connection* between "social concern and predation." The privatization of solutions to social problems improves public perception while maintaining the neoliberal policies that increased the elites' share of wealth since the 1980s, the exact same policies that caused the social problems these elites are addressing yet reproducing through charity.

The alienated aspect of the reconciliatory feeling produced by do-gooding is latent even in the highest expression of altruistic self-sacrifice: the ethical decision to abstain from reproducing. As an armchair anti-natalist, I understand the many motivations underlying this form of reconciliation. If one is childless, the thought goes, one is not responsible, or less responsible, for the many ills that plague humankind and the planet. One altruistically chooses to abstain from committing new patients to the madhouse, a madhouse hellbent on surpassing every planetary boundary. While intentional childlessness is perhaps the ultimate act of selflessness, at least one motivation for not reproducing, perhaps the paramount motivation, is an ironically quasi-Darwinian consolation: "Despite troubling social and ecological futures, I can live and die in peace because I *don't have skin in this game*. It is not my fault if the species undermines its own resource base because part of my own distinctive genetic code will pass with me, thereby protecting my own particular substance from future pain." One may reply that they are intentionally childless for various altruistic aims, but the foundation of the belief remains: consolation in the feeling that one is not personally responsible for the fate of the world.

The task, instead, is to transform the world into one in which we would not feel so guilty to bring new life into, a task that cannot be fulfilled through individual activism. The real hope for an unalienated future lives on when the social conditions that produce this kind of cognitive dissonance are brought to light instead of punching out at the dark. One should first accept one's individual helplessness in the face of monstrous social conditions. For example, instead of directing one's sympathy with the lives of sweatshop workers into a campaign for ethical consumerism, one should elevate one's sympathy into a structural analysis of the macro-level systemic workings of capitalism, a perspective that not only alters one's understanding of the lives of workers but also transforms political strategy. As elaborated upon in Žižek's (2011: 117-118) critique of modern charity, Oscar Wilde (1915: 4-6) made this argument over a century ago:

> it is much more easy to have sympathy with suffering than it is to have sympathy with thought. Accordingly, with admirable, though misdirected intentions, they [the majority of people] very seriously and very sentimentally set themselves to the task of remedying the evils that they see. But their remedies do not cure the disease: they merely prolong it. Indeed, their remedies are party of the disease. They try to solve the problem of poverty, for instance, by keeping the poor alive; or, in the case of a very advanced school, by amusing the poor. But this is not a solution: it is an aggravation of the difficulty. The proper aim is to try and reconstruct society on such a basis that poverty will be impossible. ... Just as the worst slave-owners were those who were kind to their slaves, and so prevented the horror of the system being realised by those who suffered from it, and understood by those who contemplated it, so ... the people who do most harm are the people who try to do most good [via charity]. ... It is immoral to use private property in order to alleviate the horrible evils that result from the institution of private property.

A feeling of compassion for the sufferings of the world and an altruistic desire to help should, rather than steer one to do-gooding, fuel social-structural analysis and strategies for *political* action. Political action depends on accepting, rather than fleeing, the real dissonance of the reply "Very little" to the question "What can I do?"

Readers may acknowledge that do-gooding is limited yet still engage in it because they have no hope in radical social change through political action. The reason the question is individualized as "What can *I* do?" in the first place is the absence of a collective-political project. If one accepts that do-gooding is merely a form of alienated reconciliation and if hopes for social change through political action are considered utopian, one may retreat into hiding.

Hide

Although all forms of alienated reconciliation are escapisms, *hiding* refers to what is typically meant by escapism: diverting one's awareness from consequential, important concerns by attending to less consequential, unimportant concerns or blunting the sharper discomforts of life with drugs, toys, and myth. Coupled with consumerism (see below), cynicism is perhaps the most prevalent manifestation of hiding today. This is emphasized by Žižek when elaborating the theory of cynicism as a form of ideology.

> The cynical subject is quite aware of the distance between the ideological mask and the social reality, but he none the less still insists upon the mask. The formula [of ideology] ... would then be: 'they know very well what they are doing, but still, they are doing it'. ... Cynical distance is just one way – one of many ways – to blind ourselves to the structuring power of ideological fantasy: even if we do not take things seriously, even if we keep an ironical distance, *we are still doing them*. (Žižek 1989: 29, 33)

Fatalism, cynicism's fellow traveler, has a similar structure, as discussed in chapters 3 and 6. While pessimism and nihilism often have comparable consequences, reproducing the system while ostensibly opposing it, they also offer dialectics critical moments, as discussed in chapter 6.

There are too many manifestations of hiding to cover in this section, ranging from the reemergence of communes and the identification of one's whole self with a reified tribal classification to the opioid epidemic and thousands of adults meeting at comic book conventions dressed up like fictional characters manufactured by giant corporations. Hiding is the form of alienated reconciliation highlighted in Streeck's (2016) coping/hoping/doping/shopping typology. Here I focus on two forms of hiding: (1) the continued dominance of the culture industry, including its ability to commodify flights from the inauthentic world produced by commodification ("commodified authenticity"), and (2) a new New Age "irreligious spirituality" where one embraces spiritual ideas and practices that are a product of, and implicitly affirm, the current order.

Commodified authenticity

Consumerism, taken broadly to include everything from shopping to passively gazing at the media spectacle, is an omnipresent form of hiding in overdeveloped countries due to the corporate world's powerful role in shaping our environment, from advertisements to city structure, and mind, from what we think is worthy of attention to how we think about important issues. The Frankfurt School foresaw much of this in their theory of the "culture industry," a concept with a twofold meaning: (1) culture is now a product of big business and (2) cultural products are standardized and seeming differences between products are more of the same (Johnson 2008: 121f; see Horkheimer and Adorno 1969). Media, entertainment, and advertising sell passivity, distraction, comfort, prepackaged forms of individual freedom and identity, and escape from the fears and anxieties associated with work and employment. Adorno's (2000a: 69) modification of the culture industry as the "consciousness industry" during a lecture is instructive. The term *consciousness* industry implies the production and selling of the content and form of consciousness. We are consumers first, and conscious subjects after the sale.

Developments in information and communication technology have allowed the culture industry to further seep into every crevice of life. For example, 8- to 18-year-old Americans consume nearly 11 hours of entertainment media a day (Rideout et al. 2010), and American adults consume media over 11 hours a day (Nielsen Global Connect 2018). Over $200 billion is spent on advertising expenditures annually (Griner 2017), corporations increasingly target children to create lifelong "brand devotion" (Schor 2014), and average Americans are exposed to an estimated 4,000 to 10,000 advertisements a day (Marshall 2015).

It goes without saying that what is being sold—recurring opportunities to hide from systemic contradictions—overwhelmingly foster passive compliance instead of revolutionary consciousness. Knowing that the following illustration cannot be methodologically defended, there is still some insight to be gleaned when comparing the total views of YouTube videos with substantive content to the views of those without. For example, Noam Chomsky is perhaps the most famous living left-wing intellectual. One of his most viewed YouTube videos, "Noam Chomsky full length interview: Who rules the world now?," posted May 2016, has been viewed 3.6 million times, comparable to the population of Connecticut, as of September 2020. The music video for Rhianna's pop song "Work," the most popular single when Chomsky's lecture was posted, has been viewed over a *billion* times, comparable to the population of the Americas. Perhaps it is pointless to compare a video of Chomsky, a world-renowned paradigm-shifter of linguistic theory, with a mindless snippet of peak pop culture with lyrics such as, "Work, work, work, work, work, work/ Ner ner ner ner ner ner/When you a gon' learn, learn, learn, learn, learn/Before the tables turn, turn, turn, turn, turn." Yet the most viewed YouTube video featuring Chomsky this author can locate—a recording of when he was pranked by the UK comedian Sacha Baron Cohen into an interview with Ali G, one of Cohen's satirical personalities (over 5 million views as of

September 2020)—also illustrates the prioritization and power of entertainment over thought.

One notable development in the unrelenting spread of the culture industry is *commodified authenticity*, a manifestation of hiding in which one escapes from the inauthentic reality of consumerism and commodification by buying the goods and services necessary for achieving a preformed "authentic" life. If the existentialism of old could be faulted for not recognizing that the hope for authentic spontaneity had become unrealizable and, in fact, that "[s]uch hopes are entertained simply and solely because at the moment there is no basis for hope in the objective historical trend" (Adorno 2006: 161-162), it at least strove to achieve authenticity, "the return of the individual to himself from out of alienation in the crowd" (Feenberg 2005: 85), through creative and sometimes unconventional methods. In contrast, the commodified form of existential authenticity is fully integrated with the culture industry, where one, for example, attends "secret" concerts selectively advertised by corporations to manufacture an aura of undergroundness (Sullivan 2007).

The #vanlife "movement" (i.e., social-media trend) is a clear illustration of commodified authenticity (see Monroe 2017). Vanlifers remanufacture a pseudo-minimalist hippie van culture, with every step of the journey posted on social media, complete with its own hashtag, #vanlife. The classic VW van is prized in part because "it was going to look great in the photos," as a founder of #vanlife put it (Smith quoted in Monroe 2017). Vanlifers have managed to make their journeys into salaries through such means as product placements in their social media posts. Perhaps this is the very telos of #vanlife, erected out of its origins. The initial "project" of the entrepreneurs of the #vanlife hashtag was entitled "Where's My Office Now": "We wanted to see if it was possible to combine this nomadic hippie life with a nine-to-five job" (Smith quoted in Monroe 2017).

Commodified authenticity is the highest expression of what Adorno sees as the "false reconciliation" of ego and id in the seeming permissiveness and freedom of "late" capitalism (Jarvis 1998: 83f), condensed today in the already passé hashtag #YOLO (You Only Live Once). Due to the universality of the culture industry, the reminder that death is inevitable in #YOLO is reducible to one message: purchase as many experiences as possible during your short vacation on Margaritaville Earth. Like ethical consumerism, commodified authenticity demonstrates that there is no escape from the culture industry due to the powers of commodification. Every exit is an entrance. Even spiritual exodus is a homecoming to alienation.

Irreligious spirituality

Frisk and Nynäs (2012) argue that the defining contemporary transformations in religion – fundamentalism and New Age movements – are best understood as a reaction to the rapid social changes associated with neoliberal globalization. The inherent relativizing process of globalization undermines the ability to justify particularistic worldviews. Fundamentalism is an attempt to reassert particularism. In contrast, New Age thinking and its influence on established religions reflect the neoliberal cultural context of change, namely the strong emphasis on individual choice and experience, so long as the latter involve monetary transactions. I use the term "irreligious spirituality" to refer to these status quo-friendly, profit-driven, and market-savvy spiritual and ostensibly religious movements and lifestyles that preach individual success, self-actualization, and positive thinking as opposed to self-discipline, self-purification, and piety. Irreligious spirituality is highly individualized and instrumental, practiced to achieve personal comfort and worldly goals. It is an "irreligious" spirituality because it is drained of the ethical and social demands of religious conceptions of the transcendent. While religion has long been pointed to as the archetype of escapism, it was still always also "a *protest* against real suffering" (Marx 1963: 43) driven by a desire for the transcendent, the "wholly other" (Clements 2013). Irreligious spirituality does away with this sublimated protest against reality and, instead of shining a critical light on the profane from the perspective of the transcendent, affirms the profane.

Some forms of irreligious spirituality claim affiliation with older established religions, such as the "prosperity gospel" of Protestant mega-pastors like Joel Osteen, yet, in theological content and practice, they encourage the affirmation of self and preach worldly success for the faithful. While there are numerous manifestations of irreligious spirituality, including online gurus, astrologers, and spiritual leaders (e.g., Schwartz 2020), one movement, pervasive in business and academic sectors, is quintessential: *mindfulness*, a $4 billion industry of concentration and attention exercises allegedly derived from Buddhism (Purser 2019).

Before the term "mindfulness" picked up steam, Žižek (2005) recognized how "New Age 'Asiatic' Thought" is the "perfect ideological supplement" to the current era's collective fear of technological futures and the inability to make sense of rapid change. The new replacement for Weber's Protestant ethic offers a solution to the birth pangs of "virtual capitalism":

[t]he way to cope with this dizzying change ... is to renounce any attempts to retain control over what goes on, rejecting such efforts as expressions of the modern logic of domination. Instead, one should "let oneself go," drift along, while retaining an inner distance and indifference toward the mad dance of the accelerated process. ... The "Western Buddhist" meditative stance is arguably the most efficient way for us to fully participate in the capitalist economy while retaining the appearance of sanity. ... It allows us to participate in it [capitalism] with an inner distance, keeping our fingers

crossed, and our hands clean, as it were. (Žižek 2005)

Similarly, Purser (2019) argues that the proliferation of mindfulness stripped of Buddhist ethics of compassion for others and the annihilation of selfishness, is a corporate-friendly tool of self-centeredness and self-discipline he terms "McMindfulness."

> [M]indfulness programs do not ask executives to examine how their managerial decisions and corporate policies have institutionalized greed, ill will and delusion, which Buddhist mindfulness seeks to eradicate. Instead, the practice is being sold to executives as a way to de-stress, improve productivity and focus, and bounce back from working eighty-hour weeks. They may well be "meditating," but it works like taking an aspirin for a headache. Once the pain goes away, it is business as usual. Even if individuals become nicer people, the corporate agenda of maximizing profits does not change. Trickle-down mindfulness, like trickle-down economics, is a cover for the maintenance of power. (Purser 2019: 20)

It is a tool of self-centeredness because the purpose of consuming mindfulness is to take care of Number One, whether one is a hedge fund manager who wants to enhance self-optimization or a drone pilot hoping to de-stress after the latest kill (Purser 2019: 13, 17).

McMindfulness is a disciplinary tool because it teaches workers concentration skills to increase productivity and optimization while, in leisure time, helping to relieve the stresses caused by hard work. The message that all suffering is "in your head" may even make this objectively stressful world worse by encouraging practitioners to turn attention from the structural causes of harm to personal means of coping with harm, thereby reproducing and even amplifying the structural causes. It is notable that Google had trouble enrolling software engineers in mindfulness classes provided by their non-profit Search Inside Yourself Leadership Institute until they marketed the classes as instruments to enhance career success, rather than as a method to de-stress (Purser 2019: 132)

Purser's point is not that strategies to reduce personal suffering are "bad," or that those who learn to thematize formerly missed everyday wonders are deluded. Instead, his critique is immanent: mindfulness does not live up to its own aims (mitigating suffering, stress, and anxiety) because it does not recognize the structural causes of these harms. Corporate-friendly mindfulness privatizes stress and anxiety, making it harder to identify the structural causes of stress and anxiety. While all forms of alienated reconciliation are reminiscent of the ideologies of Hegel's slave, who believes he is free despite the reality of bondage, this is clearest in the case of hiding, of which the irreligious spiritual practice of mindfulness is one instance.

> The internalization of focus for mindfulness practice also leads to other things being internalized, from corporate requirements to structures of dominance in society. Perhaps worst of all, this submissive position is framed as freedom. Indeed, mindfulness thrives on freedom doublespeak, celebrating self-centered "freedoms" while paying no attention to civic responsibility, or the cultivation of a collective mindfulness that finds genuine freedom within a cooperative and just society. (Purser 2019: 21)

Conclusion: Why be a buzzkill when there is no alternative?

If people take comfort in "alienated reconciliation," why mount a critique against it? What is wrong with believing that experts and responsible politicians will eventually address climate change with new technology, feeling good about buying fairly traded coffee, or finding solace at mindfulness retreats? As stated in the introduction, the purpose of the analysis is not a moralistic condemnation of the individual; the belief that changing the individual is the path to a truer form of reconciliation is misguided. Further, I am just as prone as anyone else to pursuing alienated forms of reconciliation or to offering the mundane advice "Do what you need to do" to cope. One cannot live in the spectacle without illusion. There is no personal escape. One adapts. The point of the critique is to show that alienated reconciliation is a self-defeating contradiction, a paradox: attempts to reconcile consciousness with current social conditions through justification, pseudo-activity, and hiding maintains these conditions, conditions which birthed the desire for reconciliation in the first place.

Adorno leaves contradictions unresolved in theory because they are constitutive of reality. Akin to true art, which should "[negate] the possibility of being assimilated into the world" (Bayoumi 2005: 53), he thinks the possibility of reconciliation is only kept open by showing the impossibility of true reconciliation in current social conditions. His goal is to bring to light the social bases of the contradictory nature of reality and ask the reader to avoid cheap solutions and false hope. Attempting to abolish social contradictions in consciousness or individual action masks the problem rather than pointing the way, even if indirectly, to the need for different social conditions. In short, pseudo-remedies to heal a given socially inflicted wound can be worse than the wound itself because they merely make it less visible, which diminishes the likelihood of mending the lesion, or even deepen the cut.

The critique of alienated reconciliation seems to imply that a non-alienated or genuine form of reconciliation is possible, an assumption that is questionable given the social, technological, and ecological trends discussed in chapter 1. Herein lies a tension not unlike that described by Hegel in his analysis of the unhappy consciousness (see above). This is the yearning to transcend or even leave the finite, impure, and sinful world for an infinite, pure, and righteous world despite recognizing that we cannot. Lucien Goldmann (1964) is right that the tragic tension produced by unhappy consciousness is one historical precedent to dialectical thought (see Cohen 1994: 162). Tragic thought juxtaposes a "radically unsatisfactory world" (Goldmann 1964: 62) to absolute values that are impossible to realize in this world, whereas dialectical thought juxtaposes this radically evil world to the *potential* for a better *future*, even if the concrete details of this world are unclear. The dialectic shares the tragic attitude's critique of dogmatism and existing social conditions, but replaces Christianity's wager on a Hidden God, "a transcendent divinity," with "an immanent wager on man's future in this world" (Goldmann 1964: 48). The following chapter explores the stacked deck against this secular wager.

Notes

1   I specify "discursive" justifications because ideology's center of gravity is in merely-lived, unreflective practices, not discourse (Althusser 1971).

2   I thank Thomas Dietz for discussions on non-reductionist approaches to evolutionary theory.

3   It makes sense that the neoliberal naturalists are attracted to the existentialists, especially Heidegger, because they too tend to reify a socially formed reality (see Adorno 1973b; Gordon 2016). Yet even Heidegger, in later years, knew that "Being" has a history.

Chapter 3

Three Flagellations of the Dialectic

Introduction: Dialectics in a nutshell

Chapter 2 is an analysis of ways in which consciousness attempts to overcome the tension between the desire for reconciliation with the world and the reality of systemic contradictions and rapid social change, strategies that are necessarily self-defeating and unsatisfying because they maintain the social conditions that produced the desire for reconciliation. The alternative to escape is to *explain* these contradictions and identify alternative possible futures already buried beneath the surface. The latter capacities require a form of consciousness called *the dialectic*, sometimes termed "ideology critique" or "dialectical thought." One goal of the book is to preserve dialectical thought despite the likelihood of catastrophe, explore ways in which we can still search for a better future, and, even if the future is grim, to locate paths to reach less undesirable conditions. This chapter summarizes what the ambiguous term "dialectical thinking" means and then describes how the dialectic, a radically historical form of thinking, lost its youthful confidence due to historical changes.

Marcuse (1960) says dialectical thought originates in everyday life with the simple recognition of the contradictions between reality and concepts, tensions ignored by common sense and unreflective approaches to science, which abstract from reality rather than attend to it. The dialectic begins with "the experience that the world is unfree; [that] man and nature exist in conditions of alienation, exist as 'other than they are'" (Marcuse 1960: ix). The dialectic preserves, rather than smooths over, unfreedom and the contradictory nature of reality in thought. It does not attempt to shake off the "experience of a world in which the unreasonable becomes reasonable and as such determines the facts; in which unfreedom is the condition of freedom, and war the guarantor of peace" (Marcuse 1960: vii) and, instead, subjects these contradictions to "negative" or oppositional thinking.

> The negation which dialectic applies to them [concepts that ignore contradictions between reality and self-definition] is not only a critique of a conformist logic, which denies the reality of contradictions; it is also a critique of the given state of affairs on its own grounds—of the established system of life, which denies its own promises and potentialities. (Marcuse 1960: vii)

There are three important moments of the dialectic suggested in this passage: the dialectic is (1) "a critique of the given state of affairs on its own grounds," (2) the assumption that the "system of life" is *established* as opposed to fixed and unchangeable, and (3) the need to uncover the "reality of contradictions" in order to reveal the order's "own promises and potentialities." (1) is often called *immanent critique*, (2) is often termed *historicization*, *denaturalization*, or *defetishizing critique*, and (3) has been termed *contradiction-crisis diagnosis* (Benhabib 1986; Gunderson 2017). I will discuss each moment in turn.

Immanent critique is a style of discourse and self-reflection that can be traced back to Hegel (2010: 512; see Antonio 1981), who argues that a refutation must:

> not proceed from assumptions lying outside the system in question and irrelevant to it. The system need only refuse to recognize those assumptions; the *defect* is such only for him who starts from such needs and requirements as are based on them.

In other words, instead of evaluating an argument from an external point of view with different starting assumptions, the dialectic encourages the given system of thought to reflect on its own assumptions in order to guide it to see its own inherent contradictions. Thus, the evaluative criterion of immanent critique is a historically given ideology under evaluation. Although most ideologies tend to contain both descriptive/ explanatory and prescriptive claims that legitimate and/or reify the social order, Benhabib (1986) helpfully distinguishes between two forms of immanent critique: categorial and normative.

Categorial immanent critique refers to the breaking down or inversion ("dialectical reversal") of established conceptual categories when confronted with reality. The concepts are shown to be self-contradictory in the sense that they cannot explain their object of analysis. Categorial immanent critique is engrained in the whole of Marx's critique of political economy, where he shows how "a free economy [turns] into monopolistic control, productive work [turns] into rigid relationships which hinder production," etc. (Horkheimer 1972: 247). The point is to expose the discrepancy between established categories of thought and the contradictions that they smooth over, thereby providing a basis for deeper analysis of the object in question. Even when there are no immediately apparent descriptive and prescriptive justifications for what is, when ideology "hardly says more than things are the way they are," the task of categorial immanent critique is to uncover the deception of the implied meaning: "it could not be otherwise than it is" (The Frankfurt Institute of Social Research 1972: 202).

Normative immanent critique "appraises society by the light of the very ideas that it recognizes as its highest values" with an awareness "that these ideas reflect the taints of reality" (Horkheimer 1947: 173). In order to avoid "normative dogmatism" yet retain value judgments, the aim of normative immanent critique is to "disclose a pervasive discrepancy between what [social institutions and activities] actually are and the values they accept. ... The ambivalent relation between prevailing values and the social context forces the categories of social theory to become critical and thus to reflect the actual rift between the social reality and the values it posits" (Horkheimer quoted in McCarney 1990: 19). For instance, in an oft-cited passage, Marx (1976: 280) declares that commodity exchange is the "very Eden of the innate rights of man. It is the exclusive realm of Freedom, Equality, Property and Bentham." But if one moves to the level of production, freedom becomes the necessity to sell one's labor-power, property becomes the ability to own another's labor-power, equality is legal equality to be exploited, etc.

Historicization, denaturalization, or, what Benhabib (1986: 21) calls "defetishizing critique" refers to a "procedure of showing that what appears as a given is in fact not a natural but a historically and socially formed reality." Ideas which lack historical self-understanding, even when relatively accurate representations of reality, are often ideological. In other words, ideology may objectively depict reality yet remain ideological because it fails to recognize the historical and contradictory nature of that reality; specifically, the recognition that ossified social forms are rooted in the activity of real concrete subjects and, thus, historically contingent and mutable. The task of defetishizing critique is to reverse this error. As Adorno (2006: 136) put it, "Marxist critique consists in showing that every conceivable social and economic factor that appears to be of nature is in fact something that has evolved historically" (see also Lukács 1971a).

Dialectical thought does not only make society "condemn itself out of its own mouth" (McCarney 1990: 20) (immanent critique) and historicize seemingly fixed and law-like conditions (defetishizing critique). It also (1) exposes contradictions and crises and (2) points to alternative social futures that may exist in present contradictions; what Benhabib (1986: ch. 4.3) calls "crisis diagnosis," though I employ a wider label: "contradiction-crisis diagnosis." I adopt this broader label only because the concepts "contradiction" and "crisis" refer to distinct, though related, phenomena and "contradiction-crisis diagnosis" addresses both. Roughly, crises are *eruptions* of contradictions, "*moments* of transformation," "*moments* of danger," whereas contradictions are persistent opposing forces that underlie crises (Harvey 2014: 4, emphases added). Again, Marx's *Capital* (1976) serves as an excellent example of contradiction-crisis diagnosis, where contradictions and crises are examined from two levels of analysis: (1) a systemic, "transsubjective," or a third "thinker-observer" perspective (i.e., the logic, movement, and "laws" of capital) and (2) an interpersonal perspective of the lived experiences of people (see also Habermas 1987: ch. 8.2). The transsubjective perspective exposes "systemic" crises and contradictions and the interpersonal perspective exposes "lived" crises and contradictions. Systemic crises and contradictions refer to those internally contradictorily elements of a system that may, over time, undermine the system itself (e.g., the contradiction between capital and the climate discussed in chapter 1), or when these elements come to a head and erupt as a crisis. Lived crises and contradictions refer to the *living-through* of systemic crises and contradictions by everyday subjects in terms of culture, practices, values, ideas, psychology, politics, and concrete social relations (alienation, exploitation, injustice, opposition, denial, confusion, etc.).

Through an analysis of how people live through systemic contradictions and crises, the second task of contradiction-crisis diagnosis is the search for emancipatory alternatives within the present. Lived crises and contradictions are the origin of both new ideological content (various ideas and practices that conceal the existence of contradictions) and the potential for a better society (in oppositional ideas, movements, and parties). The assumption throughout Hegel, Marx, and the Frankfurt School is that the present is pregnant with the future. Within its contradictions and crises, the present holds alternative futures and the normative task of the dialectician is to identity these potential alternatives and guide society in a rational direction. Dialectical thought grounds the search for alternatives in present conditions (Marcuse 1964; McCarney 1990).

Dialectical thinking assumes that "what is is fraught with tension between its empirical reality and its potentialities" (Feenberg 2005: 87). With this Hegelian supposition of a pregnant present, critical theory makes counterfactual comparisons of what is possible with what is. There is a "tension between potentiality and actuality, between what men and things could be and what they are in fact" (Marcuse 1968: 69). Dialectics elevates these antagonistic tendencies to consciousness. The goal is to help actualize more rational alternatives already possible in the current order or, at minimum, explain what restricts social alternatives. As mentioned in chapter 1, the most well-known example is Marx's contradiction between the forces and relations of production, where "the forces of production enter into the basic contradiction only as they are developed or limited by the capitalist production relations" (Young 1976: 201; see Marx 1970: 21). The practical purpose is to search for emancipatory alternatives within already existing oppositional ideas and social movements as well as technological potential.

Identifying potential alternative social futures in the present and comparing these possibilities with the actual is the essential feature of dialectical thought that separates it from the common-sensical thinking of everyday life as well as ahistorical and unreflective scientific thought. Yet the certainty and confidence in which dialectical thought could proceed in the past, assuming the inevitability or at least real possibility of a rational future, has steadily declined in response to the unfolding of recent history.[1] Because dialectical thinking is radically historical, it had to adapt to these real changes, which can be summarized as follows:

- The irrational and gory course of the twentieth century undermined teleological tendencies in dialectical thought by purging critique of the belief in the inevitable victory of freedom (the Absolute, communism).
- The cooptation of the working class through mechanisms such as the culture industry challenged the hope in a historical subject to bring about a rational society. This undermined the social-historical basis for critique and gave rise to a negative dialectics that compares the technical potential for freedom with the actuality of repression, without any expectation of realizing potentiality.
- The progressive degradation of the material environment simultaneously degrades the hope in the technical potential for a better future at all, giving rise to a catastrophic dialectics that can only compare actuality with the potential for a less bad catastrophe.

I describe these three flagellations of the dialectic below.

The first flagellation: No teleological inevitability

To oversimplify, Marx has been read in two contrasting ways, readings which reach back further to two contrasting readings of Hegel (see Jacoby 1981): (1) the "scientific" Hegel and Marx of "orthodox" Marxism, a reading with deterministic social laws, where each particularity fits into an evolving, rational totality that moves through predetermined stages toward a predetermined end, and (2) the "historical" or "critical" Hegel and Marx of "Western" Marxism, a reading with a world-making humanity shaping its own history and categories of thought, which is subject to objective structures, though structures of its own making. Orthodox interpretations of Marx have tended to stress the "necessity" of objective, historical laws culminating in communism, either through evolution or revolution. The self-assurance of dialectical thought derived from the interpretation of reality as an ultimately rational totality that, despite setbacks, contradictions, and suffering, was headed for the actualization of freedom, whether in the form of the Absolute in Hegelianism or, perhaps what is the same,[2] in the form of communism in Marxism.

Take the following passages from *The ABC of Communism*, a highly influential text of Soviet Marxism written by Nikolai Bukharin in 1919:

> from our study of the development of the capitalist system we can confidently deduce the following conclusions: The number of the capitalists grows smaller, but these few capitalists grow richer and stronger; the number of the workers continually increases, and working-class solidarity likewise increases, though not to the same extent; the contrast between the workers and the capitalists grows ever greater. Inevitably, therefore, the development of capitalism leads to a clash between the two classes, that is, it leads to the communist revolution. (Bukharin 1966: 66)

> The workers may suffer defeat in individual battles, or even in individual countries. But the victory of the proletariat is no less certain than the ruin of the bourgeoisie is inevitable. (Bukharin 1966: 137)

Or take an earlier, more reformist orthodox Marxist text, *The Class Struggle*, written by Karl Kautsky in 1892 as a theoretical and political tract summarizing the official program of the German Social Democratic Party (the Erfurt Program).

Socialist production is, therefore, the natural result of a victory of the proletariat. If the working-class did not make use of its mastery over the machinery of government to introduce the socialist system of production, the logic of events would finally call some such system into being—but only after a useless waste of energy and time. But socialist production must, and will, come. Its victory will have become inevitable as soon as that of the proletariat has become inevitable. The working-class will naturally strive to put an end to exploitation, and this it can do only through socialist production. (Kautsky 1910: 191)

There are few Marxists who defend the inevitability thesis today. In fact, it is usually invoked as a strawman to swiftly dismiss Marxism. The goal of this section is not to review the nuances of this history nor determine if this is an accurate reading of Marx's work (see Eagleton 2011: ch. 3). The straightforward point is that dialectical thought once believed that a desirable alternative world is not only possible but *inevitable*. The fact that "the attempt to change the world miscarried" (Adorno 1973a: 3), especially throughout the twentieth century, has forced the dialectic to rid itself of the idea that history will inevitably result in the Absolute.

Dialectical thought has always been informed by a continual piling up of defeats (Traverso 2017). Even if the hunt is long and vicious, the positive dialectic consoled, the taste of history chases the scent of freedom. While the Frankfurt School and others discarded the positive dialectic decades earlier (see below), Traverso (2017) identifies the Soviet Union's collapse as the final mortician of any remaining teleological assumptions that 2 centuries of defeats would inevitably sublate into the realization of a redeemed world.

While often masked by teleology, there is a rational core hidden in the modern dialectic's youthful excesses: a *choice* between socialism or barbarism, now interpreted as a wager rather than an inevitable movement toward the former (e.g., Goldmann 1964). This rational core is present even in the above "vulgar" interpretations of Marx, which do not always use the term "inevitability" as a mechanical category. A key *anthropological* assumption propped up the entire tower of materialist eschatology:

> [w]hen we speak of the irresistible and inevitable nature of the social revolution, we presuppose that men are men and not puppets; that they are beings endowed with certain wants and impulses, with certain physical and mental powers which they seek to use in their own interest. (Kautsky 1910: 90)

However, the first flagellation of the dialectic, the termination of a belief in the inevitable realization of freedom, is closely connected to the second: the possibility that the system has made men into puppets.

The second flagellation: No revolutionary subject (for now)

Although dialectical thought lost its foothold for critique in the inevitable realization of freedom, it could still rationally ground critique in the possibility of realizing a good society through real political action and social change. Marxism identifies the working class as this historical subject of change because it is the only group that is in the structural position to abolish class society, which would also be the self-abolition of the working class. The confidence in working-class revolt progressively declined throughout the twentieth century for reasons identified by Western Marxists, especially the Frankfurt School: mass conformity birthed by the manufacturing and satisfaction of "false needs" that nurture the deceptive belief that the depth of our desires, hopes, and dreams have already been met via mass consumption (Marcuse 1964) coupled with a near universalization and inversion of instrumentality (Horkheimer 1947; Horkheimer and Adorno 1969; see Jay 2016).

The culture industry, which still rules consciousness (see chapter 2), squashes the likelihood of working-class revolt because it coopts and recuperates potentially oppositional movements and ideas, promotes conformism and integration with the spectacle, and provides an escape from the fears and anxieties associated with work and employment. Along with the culture industry, human adaptation to capitalist conditions magnifies the instrumental dimension of rationality while reducing the ability to formulate substantive goals oppositional to the status quo. Capitalist productive relations shape consciousness because we must, as Lukács (1971a) details, internalize the practices and instrumental attitude necessary to survive and "succeed" (Jütten 2010). Although monopoly capitalism is—or, rather, since the neoliberal turn, *was*—characterized by a number of material benefits for many (Adorno 2003b: 102ff), survival still "depends on adaptation to a constantly changing and inherently unpredictable economic system," which conditions a calculating form of rationality (Cook 2008: 7). In Adorno, this process often goes under the heading of "self-preservation," a term meant to shine light on the fact that, despite massive gains in productivity, the species is still merely *living to survive* rather than *surviving to live* due to capitalist relations of production structured around the profit motive (e.g., Adorno 2003a: 117; see Arzuaga 2018). Along with magnifying instrumental rationality, capitalist productive relations influence consciousness and behavior through "political and social impotence." People feel powerless before the reified social world because they *are* powerless, still "appendages of the machine" (Adorno 2003a: 117).

To oversimplify the Frankfurt School's thesis: most

workers with a Netflix subscription will not rebel. In a society with ubiquitous instrumentality and conformity, as well as a corresponding lack of revolutionary consciousness, the Frankfurt School were left with a historical materialist framework without the real possibility of a fundamentally better future. The following fragments from conversations between Adorno and Horkheimer (2011: 21, 107-108, 49) in the 1950s about the prospects of updating the *Communist Manifesto* are telling:

> Max Horkheimer: "We can expect nothing more from mankind than a more or less worn-out version of the American system."

> Theodor W. Adorno: "We do not live in a revolutionary situation, and actually things are worse than ever. The horror is that for the first time we live in a world in which we can no longer imagine a better one."

> Max Horkheimer: "[I]n whose interest do we write, now that there is no longer a party and the revolution has become such an unlikely prospect? My answer would be that we should measure everything against the idea that all should be well."

The idea that a revolution was around the corner was a thesis "only stubbornness could still maintain" (Adorno 1998: 14). Comparing Marx's advantage to the Frankfurt School's position—critical theory "at the point of its greatest weakness"—, Marcuse (1964: 254-55) states:

> [t]he critical theory of society, was, at the time of its origin, confronted with the presence of real forces ... in the established society which moved (or could be guided to move) toward more rational and freer institutions by

abolishing the existing ones which had become obstacles to progress [Marx's situation]. ... Without the demonstration of such forces, the critique of society would still be valid and rational, but it would be incapable of translating this rationality into terms of historical practice [Marcuse's situation].

In the final passages of Marcuse's (1964: 257) disturbing account of consumer society, he declares that the "critical theory of society possesses no concepts which could bridge the gap between the present and its future; holding no promise and showing no success, it remains negative."

Deprived of a radical working-class movement, the dialectic increasingly portrays a stunted and deformed social world that swallows estranged and market-dependent automatons in unfulfilling and alienating work and equally unfulfilling and alienating leisure. Without the real possibility of a fundamentally better future built on social organization and revolutionary consciousness, dialectical thought reveals a grim existence of unchallenged alienation without a political means to improve the wretched lot.

As a historical method, dialectics was reformulated to account for these conditions, a "negative" dialectics (Adorno 1973a) that could still counterpose what is with what could be while "deny[ing] that there is an immanent logic to the actual that is emancipatory" and "reject[ing] precisely what Marx could still presuppose" (Benhabib 1986: 173). In these conditions, one can only expose and challenge the "irrationality of the current society ... by the 'negative' possibility of a truly rational alternative" (Jay 1973: 61). Negative dialectical thinking customarily avoids campaigning for clear alternative social futures or programmatically identifying pathways for achieving these alternatives. This avoidance is not out of dogmatic principle, but for the above specific social and historical reasons that closed off avenues for qualitative social change.

Because immediate political action is lucky yet blind at best and dangerous at worst, the Frankfurt School's assessment still informs yet haunts the search for a better world; we can only keep the possibility of alternatives open through oppositional thinking. The argument runs as follows: "political action that is not grounded in extensive thought and self-reflection risks, by its refusal of critical distance, perpetuating the very repressive conditions it seeks to change. Thinking, therefore, is ultimately a more effective means of resistance than action" (Tettlebaum 2008: 133). This "negative utopianism" and emphasis on thought over practice are grounds for the common critique of the Frankfurt School's pessimism as apolitical, quietistic, and even conservative (e.g., Lukács 1971b: 9). Solty (2020) develops a more sophisticated and updated version of this common critique, arguing that the Frankfurt School wrongly predicted that Keynesian-Fordist capitalism would be the permanent form of capitalism, one in which workers were reconciled to the status quo through relatively high wages and a state that can manage all crises, a thesis that can no longer be maintained (for an overlapping far-sighted critique of Marcuse, see Mattick 1972).

Despite massive structural changes in capitalism, especially the end of the class compromise that characterized Keynesianism, and the recent reemergence of some hope through social-democratic and socialist politics (see chapter 6), conformity is still the norm and what remains of the left is fractured and unorganized. There is nothing that bears a resemblance to an international anti-capitalist movement necessary to hint at the possibility of forming a qualitatively different historical alternative that prioritizes environmental and social wellbeing. In the US, the most left-wing mass political movement in over 4 decades coalesced around the unsuccessful presidential campaigns of a social democrat. Further, the other processes of social reproduction that kept capitalism firmly in place identified by the Frankfurt School, especially the culture industry, have expanded and cemented their power. The fact that there is still no identifiable revolutionary subject despite the deepest contradictions of capitalism on full display points to the continued relevance of the Frankfurt School's pessimistic analysis. To simplify, Keynesian capitalism reconciled workers with the system through relatively high wages, welfare spending, and entertainment while neoliberal capitalism has shown, at least up to this point, that entertainment, coupled with new forms of alienated reconciliation discussed in chapter 2, may be enough. Further, if binge watching sitcoms and food banks are not strong enough anesthetics for the social body's next agonizing spasm, a right-wing authoritarian reaction is much more likely than a socialist response given current trends. This further solidifies the continuing relevance of the Frankfurt School (e.g., Abromeit 2016). Indeed, *fascistic destruction* represents the foremost alternative to justifying, "acting" against, and hiding from chaotic and scary social conditions (e.g., Fromm 1973).

Yet even if radical social change is highly unlikely in the conceivable future, negative dialectics avoids tumbling into fatalism for two reasons. First, the future is open, and history is contingent. For example, rapid and abrupt social change has occurred in the past and is possible in the future (York and Clark 2007) and sometimes revolutions are propelled forward for structural reasons (Skocpol 1979). Second, one could still draw attention to the technical potential for a better future. For example, when political conditions made the likelihood of ending starvation highly unlikely, Adorno (1998: 144) could still announce, "thanks to the present state of the technical forces of production no one on the planet need suffer deprivation anymore." The point is to illuminate that the only fetters to ending deprivation are existing productive relations. Indeed, pointing to this potential, even if indirectly, is what separates negative utopianism, though often pessimistic, from unconditional nihilism and fatalism. There is always the potential for a world free from unnecessary suffering and toil thanks to advances in the productive forces. However, due to the ecological crisis, even this modest kernel of hope that fuels negative dialectics is under threat.

The third flagellation: No savable future

Critical theorists have long worried that the "concrete potential for qualitative social transformation" is "continually being depleted" due to the stranglehold of reification, of which a lack of a revolutionary subject is one instance (Dahms 1998: 54). Yet critique, even in the form of negative utopianism, still had a rational basis because there is a real *technical potential* for utopia due to advances in productive forces (i.e., due to technological developments, humans can be freed from most unnecessary toil given fitting social conditions). The third flagellation of the materialist dialectic refers to the realization that the hope for a better future based on this technical potential is increasingly challenged by the erosion of the most basic precondition for a good life: a livable planet. (Regarding the term "livable," I recommend the reader revisit the summary of climate projections in chapter 1.)

The second and third flagellations of the dialectic are joined at the hip; we are not adequately responding to the ecological crisis due to the absence of a historical subject to realize a better society. Ineffective mainstream climate change strategies such as green growth (see chapter 2) act as a stand-in for what is necessary: "rapid and far-reaching transitions in energy, land, urban and infrastructure, and industrial systems" (IPCC 2018: 21) through radical social change. In stark contrast to the mainstream approach to climate politics is the case for an "ecological" or "climate" revolution (e.g., Foster 2009; Magdoff and Williams 2017). In a recent interview, John Bellamy Foster (2018) argues that keeping global warming well below 2°C requires nothing less than an "ecological and social revolution" and that "[t]hose who pronounce that it is already 'too late' are … not referring to whether the change is humanly possible at this point—it definitely is. Rather, they are acceding to the prevailing logic of capital and the attendant political structure, as defining the limits of what is feasible." I agree with Foster's underlying arguments that deep emissions cuts are still possible, this possibility depends on rapid and fundamental changes in social systems by challenging the logic of capital at a global level, and declaring that change is impossible is ideological. However, due to the lack of a revolutionary subject—the second flagellation of the dialectic—, the likelihood for a climate revolution is negligible. This is not to make a strawman of the case for ecological revolution. Its proponents understand the obstacles ahead. For example, in the same interview, Foster (2018) states that "[t]he worry is that by the time the catastrophic conditions are felt on a wide enough scale, and by the time people mobilize, the situation may be immeasurably worse, with much of it out of our control. That is of course our greatest fear."

Distinct from both mainstream responses to climate change and the case for ecological revolution, a third limited prescriptive response to the prospects of catastrophic climate change is pessimistic fatalism, a response more common in hushed discussions and private fears than in formal public and academic discussions. Before explaining why "pessimistic fatalism" is limited, I qualify this point because this third tendency is revealing and certainly not unreasonable. Capitalism is on a path of "creative self-destruction" (Wright and Nyberg 2015) while actively deceiving itself that this is the case (Blühdorn 2007; Stuart et al. 2020a). Further, there has been a rightward shift in global politics since the 1980s, a swing that has intensified in recent years, with some exceptions. Most frightening is the high likelihood of failing to stay within 2°C warming, let alone 1.5°C (see chapter 1). The reason Anderson and Bows (2011: 41) argue that there is "little to no chance" of even staying within 2°C is this: if we peaked emissions in 2020, which is highly unlikely, we would need to reduce carbon emissions by 10 percent a year every year after, which would result in 100 percent decarbonization by around 2035 to 2045. In comparison, carbon emissions have increased by around 10 percent since 2010 (Global Carbon Budget 2019). Staying within 2°C warming would require the "degrowth" of material and energy throughput in overdeveloped countries, which requires a smaller overall economy (Anderson and Bows-Larkin 2013). Degrowth into a steady-state economy can be achieved through desirable social reforms and a transition out of capitalism (e.g., Alier 2009; Kallis 2011; D'Alisa et al. 2014). I endorse this strategy (e.g., Stuart et al. 2020a, 2020b), and continue to endorse it here (chapter 5). However, this book was written with the high likelihood of short- and medium-term failure in mind, which could launch the Earth system into a "Hothouse Earth" scenario (Steffen et al. 2018; see chapter 1).

With such bleak prospects, we need "enlightened doomsaying" now more than ever (Dupuy 2009; e.g., see interview with Hillman in Barkham 2018; Scranton 2018). However, a pessimistic perspective can stumble into alienated reconciliation in the form of fatalism. For example, the case for creating cultural enclaves in which we can creatively come to terms with unavoidable environmental harm (e.g., Kingsnorth 2010) is perhaps the purest expression of alienated reconciliation in climate politics. Or, in a controversial and widely read piece in *The New Yorker*, the novelist Jonathan Franzen (2019) argues that because there is such little probability that warming will remain within 2°C we ought to stop pretending effective mitigation will occur and shift all attention to adapting to an inevitably catastrophic future.

The limits of climate fatalism are easy to identify in Franzen's (2019) popular piece. While there are a number of logical holes and empirical issues with his argument, the most glaring is his assumption that, if society overshoots the 2°C goal—which is very likely, though not certain—then it will be "too late" for mitigation (for critique, see Levitz 2019). Yet giving up after missing a target was not the IPCC's intention when setting targets or warning of the dangers of seemingly small differences in temperature rise (Allen 2019). As Wallace-Wells (2019a) put it:

> [climate change] is not a matter of "yes" or "no," not a question of "fucked" or "not." Instead, it is a problem that gets worse over time the longer we produce greenhouse gas, and can be made better if we choose to stop. Which means that no matter how hot it gets, no matter how fully climate change transforms the planet and the way we live on it, it will always be the case that the next decade could contain more warming, and more suffering, or less warming and less suffering. Just how much is up to us, and always will be.

This simple argument, that less warming is better than more warming, forms the normative backbone for the case against climate fatalism and underlies the arguments made in chapters 4 and 5.[3]

The problem posed by looking toward a future that is already ablaze—the third flagellation of the dialectic—will come as no surprise to the modern environmental movement. In comparison to other social movements that mobilized around the promise for a better future, the modern environmental movement has been characterized from the start by its emphasis on the potential for a future catastrophe. Yet the focus on a future catastrophe is no longer viable when catastrophe is already underway (Cassegård and Thörn 2018), a reality clearest in the plight of today's climate refugees (Klein 2019). Due to the dwindling likelihood of systemic change in the near future to address the ecological crisis and, instead, an acceleration of the forces that drive the crisis, there is talk of a "crisis of hope" in environmentalism (see Swenson-Lengyel 2017). Stuart (in review) shows through interviews with Extinction Rebellion (XR) activists that their climate activism is fueled by an active hope that grows from despair, and a pessimism that snuffs out both fatalism and passive optimism. While I see the "post-political" strategies of XR as pseudo-activity, this book is a theoretical expression of these sentiments.

One motive for writing this book is my sympathy with both the case for ecological revolution and the lure of pessimistic fatalism. What both responses share is a resolute recognition of the direness of the potential for catastrophic climate change, a recognition that does not succumb to the temptation of prescribing so-called "realistic" market solutions and techno-fixes to reduce anxiety and fear by masking irreparable socio-ecological contradictions. However, I think both approaches are limited. The primary limitation of the case for ecological revolution is the unlikelihood of revolution due to processes described in the preceding section. Yet I agree with the premise that radical structural changes are required to achieve deep emissions cuts. In contrast, the primary limitation of climate fatalism is its blindness to possibility and the simple truth that not all catastrophes are created equal; less warming is better than more warming and our most important political task today is to limit warming as much as possible despite the likelihood of surpassing climate targets.

Conclusion: The dialectic on life support

Described in terms of changes in a future-oriented rational hope for potential alternatives to unjust and irrational social conditions, the dialectic has lost hope in the inevitability of the realization of freedom, the likelihood of a historical subject to bring about a good society, at least in the foreseeable future, and, most recently, the very possibility of saving the future. If Goldmann (1964: 48, 300, 302) is right that the materialist dialectic is based on a "wager that, in the alternative facing humanity of a choice between socialism and barbarity, socialism will triumph" and assumes that "the finite goods and even the evil of terrestrial life ... will receive a meaning inside the framework of faith and of hope for the future," then the possibility that we may undercut the material preconditions for a livable human future, not to mention the unlikelihood of socialism in at least the foreseeable future—two closely-bound issues—pushes the dialectic back into a tragic mold.

Perhaps due to its theologically stained undercoat, there is still a secular and positive eschatological tendency in dialectical thought, despite conscious efforts to expunge a belief in teleological inevitability, to assume that paradise will follow an apocalypse, the final crisis of capitalism. However, if an apocalypse has any material, concrete expression, catastrophic climate change is a better candidate than a prolonged economic crisis, and a climate "apocalypse" will certainly not deliver a paradise. The materialist dialectic must abandon this typically unacknowledged progressive apocalypticism and take responsibility for a future that is already ablaze.

Peter Frase (2011) observes that avoiding barbarism depends on political choices made now, and correctly emphasizes that socialists must come to terms with the reality of ecological limits and the problem of climate change. Rather than abandon hope, and, with it, the dialectic, the remaining chapters argue that we must continue to adapt the driving force of dialectical thought, searching for rational social alternatives within current contradictions with the hope of actualizing utopia, with dark times. How can one defend the hope for utopia while simultaneously declaring that the future is likely unsavable? As

Arias-Maldonado (2019: 7) put it: "What kind of utopias can be produced in a context where inhabitability and thus survival looks increasingly utopian? The answer is straightforward: utopias of survival or negative utopias where a *better* life cannot be dreamt of – only *a* life." Our wager today is between a world with average global temperatures that are "incompatible with an organized global community" (Anderson quoted in Roberts 2011) and a less harmful catastrophe. If dialectical thought could once hope for the realization of heaven on earth, the following chapter proposes a more modest goalpost to guide the utopian spirit in dark times: a less bad dystopia.

Notes

1   Of course, dialectical thought precedes recent modern history and the minds of Hegelians and Marxists. For a philosophical "prehistory" of the dialectic, see Kołakowski (2005: 10ff).

2   In Hegel, the Absolute is not an existing harmony, but the result of the end of a process of historical development in which we attain "a kind of unity of the free subject with the world and with all other subjects" (Krasnoff 2008: 58).

3   I would like to thank Diana Stuart and Jonathan Levy for conversations surrounding this topic.

Chapter 4

Utopianism Buried Between Catastrophes

And as with the future, so also with the past; the less we know of
either the better for our mental tranquility.
Charles J. Dunphie (1876: 28)

Introduction: Iconoclastic utopianism

This chapter explores if utopian thought is possible today,
facing the prospects of ecological catastrophe in the future
while another catastrophe breathes down its neck: human
history. By the question "Is utopian thinking still possible?" I
mean a form of anticipatory consciousness whose "perennial
aim is to resist the liquidation of the possibility of really new
experience" (Jarvis 1998: 222), the recognition "that utopian
possibilities are established in the concreteness and openness
of the material of history" (Bloch 1971: 172), or "a belief that
the future could fundamentally surpass the present" (Jacoby
1999: xi-xii). This form of utopianism is not the kind criticized
by Marx, including blueprints of a perfect world or projecting
the taken-for-granted into the future (see Eagleton 2016; chapter
2), but, instead, is precisely what was advocated by Marx: an
analysis of what social futures are latent in present society yet
fettered from actualizing.

Jacoby (2005) draws a contrast between "blueprint"
utopianism, which has run its course, and "iconoclastic"
utopianism, which is still defensible. The iconoclastic current
of utopian thought "[dreams] of a superior society but," in
contrast to the blueprint current, declines "to give its precise
measurements," disciplining itself to only speak of the future in
"hints and parables" in order to preserve the possibility of utopia

(Jacoby 2005: xv). Here, utopia is a "negative" (Jameson 2004) or "regulative" concept, an unrealizable prospect that functions as "a perennial corrective against any claim that a natural or equitable social order had been finally achieved" (Jarvis 1998: 218). This form of "anti-utopian utopianism" (Jacoby 2005: 85) is a defining feature of the dialectic.

Facing catastrophic climate change, utopian thinking is confronted with a paradox: either refashion radical ecologist visions from a past, more radical age—which ring hollow in current political conditions—or promise that the conditions that produced climate change can be improved through technological fixes (i.e., the utopia of continuing the status quo discussed in chapter 2) (Arias-Maldonado 2019). This paradox becomes more pronounced and multiplies when one's anticipatory, future-oriented gaze simultaneously drifts to the past, gazing into the boundless horrors of human history. These two topics—the catastrophe of human history and the likely future of catastrophic climate change—are relevant to utopian thinking because the latter is constituted by dual temporally-bound hopes: that the future be freed from unnecessary suffering and realize freedom and justice—in a word, *saved*—and that the past be *redeemed* in some way. The theological terminology is purposeful as the utopian tradition has historical roots in religious thought, especially Judaism (Jacoby 2005) and Christianity (Bloch 1986), or, as Marxists would have it, theology is an alienated manifestation of untapped human potential, real tendencies that are, when sociologically and historically interpreted, more logically voiced in the dialectic.

As Max Weber (1946: 280) identifies, the desires for redemption and salvation are common themes in religion, which have been intellectualized into various "world images":

[o]ne could wish to be saved from political and social servitude and lifted into a Messianic realm in the future of this world;

or one could wish to be saved from being defiled by ritual impurity and hope for the pure beauty of psychic and bodily existence. One could wish to escape being incarcerated in an impure body and hope for a purely spiritual existence. One could wish to be saved from the eternal and senseless play of human passions and desires and hope for the quietude of the pure beholding of the divine. [Etc.]

Ernst Bloch, a thinker featured heavily in chapter 5, saw the "religious expression *par excellence*," embodied in Christianity, as the "hope-laden dissatisfaction which spurs man on towards the future," and that Christianity's greatest gift to humanity, later embodied by revolutionary movements, is the capacity, or at least the will to acquire, "a way of seeing things from the perspective of the future, what they could become" (Cox 1970: 13). He calls the latter way of seeing things *the principle of hope*, which reaches its fullest and most rational expression in Marxism (Bloch 1986: vol. 3). Although utopian thinking has affinities with metaphysics and theology, it is only because these perspectives and their concepts emerge from a common human experience. Utopian thought sets itself apart as rational insofar as it is based on the analysis of social and technical *potential*: What social futures are possible or already germinal in the current social order?

Following Marx, members of the Frankfurt School were dedicated to the analysis of potentiality, contrasting what exists with what could be. However, their approach differed from Marx's due to changing social conditions (see chapter 3). Following the rise of fascism, the Second World War, the Holocaust, the control of Western consciousness by the culture industry, the crushing disappointments of state "socialism," and the all-around contraction of reason to pure instrumentality, the principle of hope found expression in what Gur-Ze'ev (1998) calls "negative utopianism" which, as Adorno (1967a) describes the thought of his friend, Walter Benjamin, keeps "fragmented hope" alive by creating a negative distance between one's consciousness and reality to reveal the "chasm" splitting utopia from what is. As explained in chapter 3, the Frankfurt School's negative utopianism always assumed that, even if human emancipation is unlikely in the foreseeable future, the technical potential for a qualitatively better future is always possible. Utopian thought could still assume the possibility of a liberated future, the secular rendition of salvation, because it was free from the burden of the prospect of catastrophic climate change, a burden confronted here.

In what follows, I first address a central concern of negative utopian thought that figures prominently in the writings of the Frankfurt School's friend, Walter Benjamin: the desire to redeem past victims of human history. Then I analyze the challenge that the likelihood of catastrophic climate change poses for a consistent theme in all utopian thought: the hope to save the future.

The hope to redeem an irredeemable past

This section addresses the thorn in the rear of utopianism: the problem of the immeasurable and ineffable suffering that characterizes human history, including the suffering of animals in human society, much of which remains untold and forgotten, and this history's relation to the goal of developing a rational society. I focus on the hope for redeeming the past through social remembrance, a motif in the work of the Frankfurt School and, especially, Benjamin. The simple argument here is this: a dedicated concrete program to collectively remember the sufferings of the past in any detail would likely be psychologically unbearable for participants. While Benjamin is right that a utopian condition would seek to redeem the past, redemption obliges the future to make good on their predecessors' hope to save their successors. Redeeming the past's hope for their successors' salvation may require that a less bad future society forget the unjustifiable and ineffable horrors of history, or, better, view the past from a new perspective, because the grief-stricken knowledge of the past's sufferings would undermine freedom and wellbeing, prerequisites for salvation. In short, if the task of redemption is cognizing the sufferings of history without rationalizing or justifying the pain, some level of social amnesia and/or a qualitatively different philosophy of history would be necessary to redeem the past's work done for the future to be saved.

There is a rather curious yet consistent strand of anti-theodicy in the Frankfurt School, who opposed justifications for the catastrophe of history with the promise of a future utopia, a line of argument that rejects rationalizations of the fact that individuals "are sacrificed and abandoned" for the whole, as does Hegel's (1956: 33) theodicy of history. In 1937, the early Horkheimer (1972: 251) states that "even after the new society shall have come into existence, the happiness of its members will not make up for the wretchedness of those who are being destroyed in our contemporary society." The most positive utopian book written by any theorist associated with the Frankfurt School, Marcuse's *Eros and Civilization* (1955: 216), closes with the following grim reflection: "even the ultimate advent of freedom cannot redeem those who died in pain. It is the remembrance of them, and the accumulated guilt of mankind against its victims, that darken the prospect of a civilization without repression." In Adorno (1973a: 361ff), any theodicy, secularized or not, is impossible after Auschwitz: it would be *obscene* to interpret the Holocaust "as a necessary moment on the path to redemption" (Houseman 2013: 168; see Skirke 2020). The Frankfurt School agrees with Hegel (1956: 33) that "[t]he History of the World is not the theatre of happiness." However, instead of siding with the whole—society and its accomplishments as a total system—they sided with real individuals, whose "blood and misery stick to the triumphs of society" (Horkheimer 1974: 66). Like Ivan Karamazov's rebellion against the promise of religious redemption due to his solidarity with the suffering wrongly justified by Providence, the Frankfurt School returned their ticket for the promised redemption of Progress.

The catastrophe of history and the desire for redemption weigh heavily on Benjamin. In what can be read as a historiography for historical materialists, Benjamin's last work "Theses on the philosophy of history" inverts two traditional interpretations of Marxist theory (Beiner 1984): (1) history, neither intelligible nor progressive, is, instead, fragmented, catastrophic, and even in "eternal decline" (Wolin 1980: 80), and (2) the historical materialist's aim is not to save the future, but, instead, to redeem the past. These inversions are interrelated, built through a critique of "historicism," a word Benjamin uses to describe a teleological theory of progress embodied by the German Social Democratic Party, such as the Erfurt Program (see chapter 3). Regarding (1), Benjamin believes the essence of history is to perish (Wolin 1980: 80) and sees the "storm" of progress as "blowing *from* Paradise" (Benjamin 1968: 257, emphasis added). He thinks that the progressivist's view leads to a complicit contemplation rather than a revolutionary urgency, an urgency nurtured by the view of history as precarious (Beiner 1984: 427).

Benjamin's anti-theodicy is related to the second inversion of traditional interpretations of historical materialism: that our aim should be to redeem the past rather than save the future. He thinks justifying past harms undermines the motivation of historical materialism, which is to take the viewpoint of the defeated. In contrast, the progressive view of history encourages radicals to disremember past generations in order to confidently look to the future: "[i]n its anxiety to liberate the grandchildren, the progressivist ideology risks alienating us from the sufferings of our downtrodden ancestors, who cannot be liberated, but at best, simply remembered" (Beiner 1984: 429). We should not justify past suffering by, for example, rationalizing the defeat of a revolution by explaining how a more radical, organized, etc. movement will advance to overpower the counter-revolution. Instead, a past-oriented utopianism allows for a "redemptive critique" (see Habermas 1979), memorably put by Benjamin (1968: 260) when describing what the working class should attend to: "the image of enslaved ancestors rather than that of liberated grandchildren."

Why and how should utopian thought focus attention on redeeming oppressed ancestors rather than liberating grandchildren? Regarding the question *why*, Benjamin (1968: 255) thinks that the "spark of hope" is fanned not by imagining a saved future but by turning attention to a "vanquished past that resists domination" (Beiner 1984: 426). The point of searching for alternative social futures is to recognize "a revolutionary chance in the fight for the oppressed past" (Benjamin 1968: 263). Each generation is supposedly "endowed with a *weak* Messianic power" (Benjamin 1968: 254) and the historical materialist "sees history as living and throbbing with revolutionary possibilities, and strives to establish a messianic relation with the past" (Beiner 1984: 428). I think Benjamin is right that the history holds sparks of hope, a topic taken up in chapter 5.

Regarding the technical question concerning *how* to redeem the past, the short answer is *remembrance*. Worthen (1999: 263-264) describes Benjamin's notion of remembrance as a past-oriented form of attention that:

[discloses] the discontinuities of history, the broken promises, the crushed desires, and by grasping these transfigure the present with the light of the Messianic. Redemption becomes manifest through remembrance, which still holds the power momentarily to interrupt "the one single catastrophe" that the angel of history beholds, while redemption's most lethal enemy is that forgetfulness which dreams its amnesia as progress. (cf. Houseman 2013: 167)

The rest of this section takes seriously Benjamin's articulation of the "possibility of a radical break with the continuum of history experienced in society under capitalism" (Worthen 1999: 266), asking two naïve questions: (1) What would redemption through remembrance look like as a concrete program? (2) Is such a program possible and/or desirable? The goal is not to construct a blueprint of redemption as remembrance, but to force utopian thinking to stay within the bounds of the anthropologically possible.

Intolerable collective memory

While Benjamin's aim is not to programmatically describe what redemption through remembrance would look like, it is a question that should be considered, even if the answer is tentative and speculative. What is redemption if we assume that "only for a redeemed mankind has its past become citable in all its moments" (Benjamin 1968: 254)? In a thesis built on a poem written by Benjamin's friend Gershom Scholem about Benjamin's Paul Klee painting, *Angelus Novus* (see Handelman 1991), Benjamin famously allegorizes history as a past-facing angel blown forward by the "storm of progress," and remarks that, "[w]here we perceive a chain of events, he sees one single catastrophe which keeps piling wreckage upon wreckage and hurls it in front of his feet. The angel would like to stay, awaken the dead, and make whole what has been smashed" (Benjamin 1968: 257). If a symbol of a redeemed condition is the angel of history ceasing the storm of progress and "mak[ing] whole what has been smashed," the only imaginable actualization of this state would be a human society that is collectively conscious of history as a prolonged "single catastrophe."

For Benjamin, remembrance would target two specific

"lost experiences": (1) the "victims of progress" and (2) the "primitive communist" societies "that the storm of progress has removed from us" (Löwy 1992: 118). The latter form of romantic remembrance, influenced by reading Johann Jakob Bachofen, is not the focus here. Instead, I concentrate on what a remembrance of the experiences of victims of progress may require, arguing that attaining the perspective of the angel of history may be too agonizing to tolerate. The argument is not that past sufferings, hopes, disappointments, and oppositional ideas should be forgotten in our attempt to create a livable world, for their memory can illuminate the possibility of a less bad world (see chapter 5). Nor do I challenge the idea that the dreams and defeats of the past can kindle contemporary hope, a mnemonic relation that should continue inspiring the left's political imagination (e.g., Traverso 2017). These are some of Benjamin's enduring insights. Instead, the argument, built on a more literal reading of Benjamin, is that the goal of redeeming the past through an exhaustive remembrance of the defeated may be psychologically intolerable and, further, that the hopes of the defeated may counsel against this path to utopia.

Imagine a best-case scenario in which a program to collectively remember the past victims of progress is adopted strictly to redeem or do justice to the past, and not used for nationalist aims (Rieff 2016), to deny conflictual and violent histories to inspire unity in civil bodies, or to achieve other cases of "abuses" of memory and forgetting (Ricoeur 2004). Let us assume that the aim was pure: to commensurate the vanquished. Let us also assume that humanity had suspended the typical "bourgeois coldness" to suffering (Adorno 1973a: 363) and looked to the past with a soft heart and a refusal to justify the battlefields, factories, bloodshed, torture, and wasted lives. With these assumptions, I think that if we viewed the past from the perspective of the vanquished with the initiative that "nothing that has ever happened should be regarded as lost for history" (Benjamin 1968: 254), then the gaze would be too unbearable to endure. To retell billions upon billions of stories of innocent humans and nonhumans who lived and died in pain due to structural conditions that left basic needs unfulfilled despite the technical potential to meet them, the stories of those who were harmed for arbitrary and irrational social norms, as well as the stories of those who were deliberately damaged through purposeful starvation, rape, execution, burnings, etc.— there would be no "etcs." in such a project—, may do more than just "darken the prospect" for flourishing in a utopia (Marcuse 1955: 216).

There is little evidence that history is a process of humanity's intersubjective self-realization. Yet if a collective owl of Minerva emerges in the future, a higher-order retrospective eye free of theodicy, it would uncover a slaughterhouse so gory and pointless that the collective subject—if it does not *give up* and resign from the world (von Hartmann 1931, vol. 3)—would have two remaining options: *turn away* or *learn*. By "turn away," I mean that the never-ending tales of disappointment, dejection, exploitation, suffering, and cruelty would encourage a return to social amnesia, to snuff out the owl of Minerva and look away from the past. By "learn," I mean that it is possible to imagine such a project serving a non-theodic yet educative function. I briefly discuss each possibility in turn.

One possible outcome for a collective remembrance of history without theodicy is a purposeful return to social amnesia. If humanity attained the perspective of Benjamin's angel, the lucidity would be intolerable, and we would strive to return to darkness. The assumption that total recollection is unbearable is not new. Emil Cioran (1973: 38-39), for example, claims that "[w]ithout the faculty of forgetting, our past would weigh so heavily on our present that we should not have the strength to confront another moment, still less to live through it. Life would be bearable only to frivolous natures, those in fact who do not

remember." David Rieff (2016: 145) too argues that life would
be impossible without forgetting: "without at least the option
of forgetting, we would be wounded monsters, unforgiving
and unforgiven ... and, assuming that we have been paying
attention, inconsolable." Similarly, the great sociologist Peter
Berger argues that "human actors prefer reification to anomie,
because the former offers comfort through amnesia" (Turner
2001: 111). The fact that one's life experiences are simply too
painful to remember, or remember clearly, is also one of the
starting points of psychoanalysis. Note that these accounts
focus on the psychological necessity of forgetting the details of
one's own short *personal* history. If we cannot bear looking at
our own relatively brief lives in the face, the demand that we
remember the sufferings of history is surely too tall an order,
even if the future ushers in a New Man. If redemption involves
a social effort to remember the horror of human history with
some concrete detail from a perspective that does not reify or
legitimate socially unnecessary suffering, the content would
be psychologically excruciating, producing insufferable grief,
sadness, and guilt.

There is a silver lining in the argument that it would be
unbearable to see history as does Benjamin's angel; it seems
unlikely that the past victims of progress would *want* their
suffering to be remembered, unless such a remembrance was
beneficial for the future. There is a contradiction in Benjamin's
insistence that utopian thought ought to focus attention
on redeeming oppressed ancestors rather than liberating
grandchildren: What of the many cases of our oppressed
ancestors who desired to liberate their grandchildren? While
the hope to liberate grandchildren is spurned by Benjamin, it is
common (for examples, see the following section). If redemption
means anything it means actualizing the thwarted desires and
hopes of predecessors. Thus, a redeemed condition would also
need to make good on the past's desire for a better future. It is

because predecessors want their successors to live happily that their successors, if they are motivated to redeem the hopes and desires of the past, should strive to live happily, which would entail some selective historical amnesia or, alternatively, a new philosophy of history that is neither theodic nor tragic.

The thought that redeeming the past would mean realizing our predecessors' goal to make a better future for their successors brings us to another possible reaction to a lucid look at the catastrophe of history: a new philosophy of history. By a "new" philosophy of history, I mean one that seeks to interpret history in a light that stays true to our predecessors' desire for the future to live happily. Yet, again, theodicy is off the table. Even a transitory remembrance of one genocide, war, or other atrocity with an honest resolve to put one's self or a loved one in the life of a single victim is to know that it would be better if we stayed in the trees. If the perspective of cosmic time and space discloses the futility of all action, then the perspective of the victims of progress discloses human history's unjustifiability. However, if our successors should find themselves in a rational society, they should feel free to live without guilt and grief about the catastrophe of history because redeeming the vanquished would mean satisfying their wish for a saved future.

If this account seems too abstract to be of any use, I ask the reader to consider the following questions: Do you desire the future of humanity to be free? If so, would you want your liberated grandchildren, biological or not, to burden themselves remembering your deepest sufferings and injustices done to you? I suspect not. Few thoughts are more troubling. And if you desire for your liberated grandchildren to remember your sufferings and experiences of injustice, it is likely for a pedagogical purpose, to learn lessons from these experiences. What lessons? The future, if it is not as terrible as the present, should see the current era as a backward and horrible age, where humans were either fired or forced to continue working during a pandemic, houses were left vacant despite homelessness, even on the coldest nights, and one could be put behind bars for life for petty theft (Holpuch 2020). We should hope that the present is nearly incomprehensible to the future. Due to the humanly produced and immaterial yet real pseudo-natural determinants of an unreflective social "second nature," the ruthlessness of the present age, if it can be fathomed at all, may be understood by reflective successors in a way analogous to how we currently interpret the act of one forest animal eating another. While the owl of Minerva would be left without a sound justification for the temporal abattoir called history, the future may be able to learn without rationalization or fixation. After learning lessons from the study of an unjust prehistory, I suspect we want our liberated grandchildren to forget us, or at least learn and live with our forgiveness. I find few thoughts more comforting than for current and past sufferings, including my own, to "disappear irretrievably," against Benjamin's (1968: 255) wishes, so the future may be happier. Unfortunately, a happy future may be a material impossibility due to a second emerging catastrophe: accelerating ecological crises, most notably catastrophic climate change.

The hope to save an unsavable future

The previous section explained why the burden of historical suffering is not necessarily a stranglehold on utopian thought. This section explores a future-oriented thorn in utopianism: the ecological crisis, focusing on the likelihood of catastrophic climate change. If the horror of human history dug a grave for the possibility of utopia, then the prospect of catastrophic climate change kicked it in and began shoveling dirt. Due to the likelihood of catastrophic climate change, the hope for salvation, long pejoratively termed "utopian" in the sense of unfeasible, may turn out to be utopian in the sense of a technical impossibility. After explaining what I mean by the hope for salvation and discussing its role in utopianism, this section examines Adorno's negative definition of progress as catastrophe-prevention and its relevance to the likelihood of catastrophic climate change.

By "hope for salvation" I mean the "hope that within the greater march of time the work of one's life contributes to building a humane society" (Terreblanche 2008: 890) expressed in "a devotion to human liberation" (Bloch 1986: 1182). The secular hope for salvation is akin to the early Horkheimer's evidently positive description of the materialist motivations for building a humane society, contrasted with the idealist's theistically-rooted motivation to give this task an absolute meaning. In comparison to theism's offshoots:

> [a] theory derived from the classical and the French Enlightenments ... holds that the world contains no inherent meaning ... Whoever accepts this theory does not link its corresponding existential demands with an eternal, spiritual being. ... When things are going well, later generations will remember the martyrs who died for freedom. However, this will mean ... absolutely nothing [to the martyrs]. However, this knowledge in no way provides action with a narrower horizon. ... As long as the goals that determine his own life do not crumble along with him, but rather can be pursued in society after his death, he may cherish the hope that his death will not mean the end of his will. The goal of self-realization is not, for him, contingent on his status as an individual, but rather is dependent on the development of humanity, and the end does not appear to him merely as destruction. (Horkheimer 1993b: 157-158)

In other words, the materialist's motivation for striving to save the future springs from the desire for humanity to reach self-realization, a secular hope devoid of higher meaning, rooted in the human will.

Yet the materialist's hope for salvation is perhaps better described as secular*ized* rather than secular. Bloch (1972: 268-269) argues that the "What-for" or the "distant goal" of the Marxist method of ideology critique and political-economic analysis is "unquestionably rooted in the originally Christian ground-plan for the 'Kingdom of Freedom' itself." Fromm (1966: 121ff) too links the socialist hope for a humane society to the Christian hope for heaven, though one that must be made real on earth. He defines hope as a paradox, an "attitude which visualizes salvation occurring right at this moment, yet it also is ready to accept the fact that salvation may not come in one's own lifetime, and maybe not for many generations to come" (Fromm 1966: 121). He warns against the tendency of the hope for salvation to stagnant into a "passive waiting" for a predetermined great future to rise out of, for example, the "laws of history" (cf. Macy and Johnstone 2012). Fromm uses the following speech by Robespierre as an example of passive waiting:

O posterity, sweet and tender hope of humanity, thou art not a stranger to us; it is for thee that we brave all the blows of tyranny; it is thy happiness which is the price of our painful struggles; often discouraged by the obstacles that surround us, we feel the need of thy consolations; it is to thee that we confide the task of completing our labors, and the destiny of all the unborn generations of men! (Robespierre quoted in Fromm 1966: 122).

While Robespierre's hope for future salvation is present in all utopianisms worthy of the name, Fromm is right to remind us that a teleological belief that Things Will Get Better can have dangerous implications, including Stalinism's justification of terror for the sake of History's predetermined stages.

Additionally, as discussed above, we should be skeptical of the teleological belief in progress due to the unjustifiable horrors of history. The unfolding of history itself (e.g., the Holocaust) has disproven the "magic spell" (Adorno 2006) of the traditional notion of progress as an "irresistible" and "automatically pursued" teleological progression from prehistory to utopia (Benjamin 1968: 260). As Adorno (1973a: 320) put it, "[n]o universal history leads from savagery to humanitarianism, but there is one that leads from the slingshot to the megaton bomb." This insight not only has important implications for relations with our predecessors, as explained in the previous section, but also for relations with our successors.

Damaged reconciliation: For a less bad future

Drawing from Adorno, this subsection argues that a socially achieved damaged reconciliation with nature is a rational goal to motivate utopianism in an era in which ecological degradation is undermining a previously taken for granted requirement for a better alternative future: humanity's life support system. In a political climate in which utopian thought has been "stone dead" for decades (Jacoby 1999: xii; Žižek 2016), the reader may reply to the idea of achieving reconciliation with nature through social change with the typical cold yet reasoned retort: "That's utopian." On the one hand, it is misleading to use "utopian" as a pejorative when "That's utopian" is meant to describe "projects for social change that are considered impossible," because "impossible" in this context almost always actually means *unfeasible* (Marcuse 1970: 63). "That's utopian" as in "That's unfeasible" is misleading because (1) unfeasibility "shows itself only after the fact" and, (2) even if subjective and objective factors for realizing a better world are absent or immature, these factors may be developed *during* a transition: "[a]ll of the material and intellectual forces which could be put to work for the realization of a free society are at hand" (Marcuse 1970: 63,

64). This question is taken up in chapter 5. However, "utopian" as a pejorative label still accurately applies to any project that strives to break natural laws (e.g., the goal of eternal youth) (Marcuse 1970: 63) and, today, for any political project that seeks to actualize universal human freedom in a severely degraded natural environment. Adorno's thinking is helpful here because he develops interrelated negative and positive formulations of reconciliation—the end of what is currently called "progress" and the remembrance that humans are natural beings—that highlight rather than conceal this problem.

Like the rest of the first-generation Frankfurt School, Adorno argues that rationalization, a goal originally intended to free humanity from nature's supremacy, had paradoxically enslaved humans along with the rest of nature (Horkheimer and Adorno 1969; for the Frankfurt School's application for human-nature relations, see Leiss 1974; Mills 1991; Eckersley 1992; Vogel 1996; Biro 2005, 2011; Cook 2011; Nelson 2011; Gunderson 2015b, 2016; Stoner and Melathopoulos 2015; Luke 2020). What is considered progress in Western civilization "runs in a single strand, on the rails of the mere domination of nature" (Adorno 1998: 212), a rationality "reproduced" in society and the self, creating a condition in which "the material preconditions for a free society have been created [i.e., the forces of production] [yet] the subjective conditions for its realization [i.e., revolutionary consciousness] ... have been distorted" (Whitebook 1979: 42, emphasis removed). The beginning of real progress would entail the end of progress as conventionally understood as endless production for the sake of production and endless consumption for the sake of consumption. Whereas traditional progress is the continual expansion of capital accumulation and the instrumentalization of reason, real "progress would consist in preventing or avoiding catastrophe by disrupting the domination of nature that has characterized much of human history" (Cook 2008: 45).

In his critique of liberal optimism, on the one hand, and the empty "progress-bashing" among existentialists, on the other (Hohendahl 2013), Adorno (1998; 2006) develops a "negative" theory of progress. A negative theory of progress does not mean a simple rejection or inversion of the modern notion of progress, as the very goal of critique is to achieve progress (O'Connor 2008: 181; see also Hohendahl 2013). Critique today, however, is not founded on a belief in a predetermined better future (see chapter 3), but, instead, on "the hope that the earthly terror does not possess the last word" (Horkheimer 1973: xiv). Progress today is measured by:

> whether humanity is capable of preventing catastrophe. The forms of humanity's own global societal constitution threaten its life, if a self-conscious global subject does not develop and intervene. The possibility of progress, of averting the most extreme, total disaster, has migrated to this global subject alone. Everything else involving progress must crystallize around it. Material needs, which long seemed to mock progress, have been potentially eliminated; thanks to the present state of the technical forces of production no one on the planet need suffer deprivation anymore. Whether there will be further want and oppression—which are the same thing—will be decided solely by the avoidance of catastrophe through the rational establishment of the whole society as humanity. (Adorno 1998: 144)

Stated positively, this conception of progress means "strengthening resistance to historical regression" (Hohendahl 2013: 246).

Adorno terms the end of the blind domination of nature "reconciliation." In positive terms, this is the aim of forming a more harmonious relationship between humanity and nature in practice by altering social conditions and, in thought, the "transformation of our relation to and knowledge of nature such that nature would once again be taken as purposeful, meaningful or as possessing value" (Whitebook 1979: 55). The concept of reconciliation does not refer to a future "messianic transformation of time," but, instead, affirms the *possibility* for a "transformation of experience" (O'Connor 2008: 186), specifically a radical change in consciousness: a collective realization that we are a part of nature. Adorno believes that if humanity came to terms with the fact that it is "just" another animal on a planet shared with other natural, finite beings, we would not only paradoxically realize our highest humanity — "we are no longer simply a piece of nature from the moment we recognize that we are a piece of nature" (Adorno 2000b: 103) —, we would also transform the course of history. Perhaps "when human beings become conscious of their own naturalness" they will "call a halt to their own domination of nature": "we might say that progress occurs where it comes to an end" (Adorno 2006: 152).

Although a critique of the naturalization of the social, which can always be changed, negative dialectics is also a critique of intellectual and collective attempts to ontologically separate humanity from nature: we are animals and subjectivity and intersubjectivity are wholly dependent on, though not determined by, natural processes (Cook 2011). We are matter. Reconciliation is a potential only after human beings collectively *remember* that they are nature too, or when nature realizes itself. In fact, Adorno's model of a reconciled human being is a reasonable animal at rest (see chapter 5).

To be clear, Adorno is not calling for a romantic "return to nature." He thinks that any attempt to overcome the contradiction between humanity and nature within existing conditions by, for example, calling for the abolition of culture, is not only impossible, but a destructive alienated reconciliation that is worse than the original tension (Jarvis 1998: 33). Further,

Adorno does not believe that there is a hidden teleology leading to reconciled conditions. Instead, he is arguing that the end of the progress of production and consumption for the sake of production and consumption requires coming to terms with our own naturalness, or, for reason to reflect on its origins in self-preservation (Adorno 1973a: 289). The future may bring about an "abolition of practice, of production for production's sake" and the realization of freedom (Adorno 1973a: 389).

The possibility that we may truly recognize ourselves as nature always remains open, though this realization may emerge only after, or even because, we have scorched our home. Hence the continued relevance of Adorno's notion of genuine progress as catastrophe-prevention through the end of "progress" as "production for the sake of production" (Marx 1976: 742). He put it this way during a lecture: "I believe that you should start by taking progress to mean this very simple thing: that it would be better if people had no cause to fear, if there were no impending catastrophe on the horizon ... For progress today really does mean simply the prevention and avoidance of total catastrophe" (Adorno 2006: 143). This is the best we can hope for the future: the "avoidance of total catastrophe."

Hoping for a less bad future in the context of climate change means, first, looking at the exceeding unlikelihood that global average temperatures will stay within 2°C, let alone 1.5°C, due to processes of social reproduction, path dependency, a dysfunctional and inadequate political infrastructure, the spectacularization of social movements, and the power of ruling interests. However, rather than throwing one's hands up in a fatalistic act—a form of alienated reconciliation—, preserving the hope for salvation as the hope for a less bad future entails focusing attention to the fact that we still have time to prevent catastrophic climate change, and, even after it is too late, we have a responsibility to make the future less bad than business as usual. *4°C is worse than 3°C! A less bad world is possible!*—slogans for an unsavable future. (For the meaning of "unsavable future," see the summary of climate change projections in chapter 1. A reminder that this book was written with the likelihood of at least short-term future failure in mind, as explained in chapters 1 and 3.)

A less bad catastrophe as the dialectic's goalpost means sustaining the hope to save our grandchildren, though realizing that "salvation" no longer means heaven on earth, but, instead, salvation from unlivable conditions. In utilitarian terms, this means pursuing the "least possible unhappiness" rather than the greatest happiness (von Hartmann 1931, vol. 3: 73). In Marxist terms, it means the crushing awareness that the future, like us, may be *stuck* in *prehistory* (Marx 1970: 22), a "still unfree" history (Marcuse 1970: 62) that is "not consciously produced" (Bloch 1976: 4), one in which humanity continues to be subjected to its own creations such as climate change.

The more modest aim of a less bad future is not a smokescreen defense of the utopian-pragmatic belief that capitalism will persist in the long-term, which is an ecological impossibility. Instead, the hope for a less bad catastrophe means that the conception of communism as the full development of productive forces, as material abundance, can no longer function as the materialist dialectic's Hidden God (Goldmann 1964). Not only would the realization of such a vision deepen rather than challenge capitalism's anti-ecological dynamics, as countless eco-socialists have pointed out for decades, but, further, future possibilities are already materially constrained and conditioned by past, present, and near-future capitalist dynamics due to their long-term environmental impacts. Depending on when carbon emissions peak and how rapidly they fall, we may face a future where extreme heat waves, floods, water and food shortages, and other hostile conditions become normative, especially for the most vulnerable. Even if communal social forms develop in response to these harsh circumstances and shortages—for example, eco-villages that are necessarily decentralized due to energy use restrictions, and perhaps collectively organized through a social-democratic global bureaucracy —, they will still unavoidably be dystopian due to especially harsh environmental circumstances and resource shortages. Here, the Hidden God of dialectical thought shifts into a catastrophe that is less bad than the more likely catastrophe: capitalism lumbering on, leading to, in the short- to medium-term, what a UN report describes as a "climate apartheid scenario" — a scenario in which "the wealthy pay to escape overheating, hunger, and conflict, while the rest of the world is left to suffer" (Alston 2019) — and, in the long-term, the extinction of the species driving the sixth extinction.

Conclusion: Dialectics trapped in prehistory

This chapter asks if utopian thinking can be salvaged given that a past of immeasurable suffering will likely culminate in catastrophic climate change. Regarding the utopian desire to redeem the past, I argue that Benjamin's demand that we tell the story of history from the perspective of the victims of progress would be an unbearable project. The closest act successors can make to redeem the past is to realize their predecessors' desire for their successors to be happy, which would require that successors either selectively forget the sufferings of their predecessors or view their suffering in a light that neither justifies nor fixates on the past. Regarding the hope for a saved future, past generations fueled by this motivation could take solace in the belief that, even if they failed to bring about a better world, the real possibility for a good society always remained. This hope shudders at the prospect of catastrophic climate change because the current system may undermine the possibility of a livable life environment, an objective precondition for a good society. Utopianism is still salvageable, though in a form that is not motivated by the desire to save the future, but to "merely" make the future *less bad*, a goal exemplified in Adorno's utopian image of reconciling relations with nature by ending what is typically considered progress: the blind domination of nature.

While the modern doctrine of progress, arising from the Christian doctrine of salvation, is no longer defensible, what is still defensible is a "commitment to the *spirit* of a utopian future" and "a *specter* of utopia" (Thompson 2016: 442). Today, keeping the utopian spirit alive, and with it, the dialectic, relies on pointing to the potential for a less bad future and a damaged reconciliation with nature. If the materialist hope for a less bad future cannot be substantiated with a teleological theory of progress, this hope, if it is rational and not mere fancy, must demonstrate that there is a *potential* for a less bad catastrophe; a qualitatively different society, one that can achieve damaged reconciliation. Chapter 5 explores the following question: On what hitch can the dialectic rationally fasten its utopian relation to the future?

Chapter 5

Anticipatory Reconciliation: Mere Possibility and Mundane Transcendence

Introduction: Negative dialectics, thawed

The previous chapter argued that, although saving the future is now an unlikely possibility, we can still reasonably hope for a future that is less bad than business as usual or business as usual with minor modifications. This chapter identifies possibilities for a less bad future and objective reasons to keep hope alive.

Anticipatory reconciliation is the dialectic's alternative to modern ways of coping with unsettling social and ecological contradictions that paradoxically reproduce the conditions that caused the desire to overcome alienation, or, modes of "alienated reconciliation" (see chapter 2). Anticipatory reconciliation refers to the consciousness of social, political, and technological possibilities inherent in current contradictions that, if expanded, present opportunities for a less bad dystopia. This form of reconciliation also includes the desire to preserve valuable aspects of the present well into the future and protect them from forces of unfreedom and destruction. It is a state of consciousness described by Harry Braverman (1998: 5) as "nostalgia for an age that has not yet come into being." In contrast to alienated reconciliation, the "reconciliation" in anticipatory reconciliation is not a reconciliation with the status quo. Instead, it is reconciliation with the *possibility* for a less bad *future*, a form of reconciliation that puts consciousness in opposition to the social forces that impede this future. Before delineating some of the conceptual puzzles involved in this formulation, it is worth discussing a thinker briefly introduced in the last chapter who influenced this line of argument, a figure credited with saving his more well-known friend, Adorno, from nihilism: Ernst Bloch (Mendieta 2005: 12).

Bloch was an exhilarating and scandalous Marxist theorist, largely ignored until the last decades of his life, who has received increasing attention in recent years (Boldyrev 2014: 1, e.g., Thompson and Žižek 2013; Eagleton 2015: ch. 3; Lerner 2015: ch. 3; Thompson 2016). He broke numerous Marxist intellectual norms, from integrating non- and even anti-Marxist traditions into Marxism, including *Lebensphilosophie*, mysticism, cabalism, neo-Kantianism, and neo-Platonism, to explicitly yet atheistically defending religion and theology as fountains of hope (Jay 1984; Goldstein 2001, 2005). One of Bloch's consistent blasphemies within the Marxist tradition is his proud identification with utopianism, though a "concrete" version, mentioned in the previous chapter, that locates "objective real possibilities" latent in current tendencies and contradictions (Solomon 1972; Hudson 1982: 99ff; Levitas 1990; Anderson 2006; see also Wright 2010).

Bloch's life was devoted to elaborating a "philosophy of hope," an ontology that directs consciousness toward *what is possible*, centering around a concept with multiple meanings: "not-yet." The "not-yet-conscious" is our "unclear and undefined awareness of our needs and potentialities which are prefigured in our daydreams and desiring" (Kellner and O'Hara 1976: 24) and anticipatory knowledge of possibilities latent in the world. The world is full of "not-yet-being," an unfinished and changeable multiverse of latent possible futures in the present that are partially formed and will either wither, remain latent until an anticipated future realization, or burst asunder due to our sharpened "theory-praxis" that helps birth a desirable future.

In comparison to Adorno's negative dialectics, Bloch's (1986: 209) dialectic of hope is less cautious about making programmatic political recommendations and erecting positive images of the future, or what he calls the "warm stream" of Marxism, which he thinks must be paired with its "cold stream" of ideology critique and political-economic analysis. However, even Adorno knew that the catastrophic implications of some problems facing contemporary societies compel the dialectician to identify imperfect solutions and alternatives that are unlikely to actualize. For example, Adorno (1973a: 365) famously advances a new historical categorical imperative rooted in dire real events: "to arrange their [humankind's] thoughts and actions so that Auschwitz will not repeat itself, so that nothing similar will happen." This imperative not only requires the cold stream of Marxist analysis, to grasp the social conditions and ideologies that are conducive to genocide, but also the warm stream of affirmative prospect exploration. In this case, Adorno (1998: 191-204) controversially recommended education and thinking (see Tettlebaum 2008: 133f). The point here is not to evaluate the soundness of Adorno's prescription, but to show that even negative dialectics requires a warm stream to stay true to its task in certain conditions.

Despite living in contradictory and near-catastrophic times, this chapter identifies two broad bases for a warmer negative dialectics: "mere possibility" and "mundane transcendence." *Mere possibility* refers to a realm of the possible that may never be actualized but still exists in the sense that some of the conditions for becoming actual are present. Bloch's in-depth treatment of the category of possibility is explained in more detail below. *Mundane transcendence* is a concept borrowed from Axel Honneth (1994: 255), who uses the intentionally paradoxical term "intramundane transcendence" to refer to the "pretheoretical resource in which its [critical theory's] own critical viewpoint is anchored extratheoretically as an empirical interest or moral experience." Whereas mere possibilities refer to potentialities that, if politicized and freed from social-economic fetters, can help form a less bad future, I use the term mundane transcendences—the "mundane" is used more specifically than Honneth probably intended—to refer to the everydayness of hopeful experiences that allow dialectical thought to carry on in dark times.

In what follows, I first, drawing on Bloch, break down the category of possibility into external ("potentiality") and internal ("capacity") forms. Following, "mere" possibility, as opposed to "real" possibility, is conceptualized by thinking through the interplay of potentiality and capacity. Then the fruitfulness of the category of mere possibility is defended on practical grounds and I explain how the concept can help elevate discussions of climate politics. After defining and briefly outlining some forms of mundane transcendences, I provide an extended illustration concerning the hope we find in observing animals at rest.

The possible

"Possibility" is a murky category, and there is a common lack of precision when the term is used. Bloch's (1986: 223ff) four-part typology of the "layers" or "grades" of possibility is instructive: (1) the formally possible; (2) the factually possible; (3) the fact-based possible; and (4) the objectively-real possible, or, real possibility (Hudson 1982: 132ff). This section is concerned with Bloch's third layer of possibility: the *fact-based possible* (see the next section for discussion of real possibility). Unlike the factually possible, which rests on insufficient knowledge that requires "caution in judgement" (e.g., when we make hypothetical or probabilistic predictions), the fact-based possible rests on the object that is "insufficiently *emerged*," "that could become this or that" (Bloch 1986: 229). The fact-based possible refers to "the open structural or dispositional possibility of the *Gegenstand* [Object] and its states of affairs ... and taking account of its social and lawful variability" as well as "a copy of what the object can hypothetically become through variability and inter-relation" (Hudson 1982: 133). The fact-based possible is the "purely structural possibility of the propensity to something," which is "not yet the same as this real propensity itself" (Bloch 1986: 231).

Understanding the variable nature of fact-based possibilities, and crucial to the distinctiveness of this ontological category of possibility, is the distinction between the *internal* and *external* dimensions or conditions of fact-based possibilities. Although Bloch applies his categories to nonhumans as well, the *internal* dimension of the fact-based possible is usually "subjective human activity" (Amsler 2015: 107) and the "political form of active possibility is the ability of the subjective factor" (Bloch 1986: 232). He calls this internal dimension "active" possibility, "capacity" or "potency." The *external* condition of the fact-based possible refers to social, technical, and environmental factors that are partially ripe or ripe for change. He calls these conditions "passive" possibility or "potentiality." Capacity is the ability to change, direct, and "re-determine" changeable external conditions (potentiality). That is, the internal dimension, or capacity, is the "capability-of-doing-other" and the external dimension, or potentiality, is the "capability-of-being-done" or "capability-of-becoming-other."

The internal (capacity) and external (potentiality) dimensions of fact-based possibilities interact in partial fulfillment and different levels of development. For example, you cannot have a workable capacity, or a "capability-of-doing-other," without an environment and/or social structure that are changeable or "capability-of-being-done" or "capability-of-becoming-other," i.e., conditions with the potentiality for change: "without potentiality of the capability-of-becoming-other, neither the capability-of-doing-other of potency would have space, nor, without the capability-of-doing-other of potency, would the capability-of-becoming-other of the world have a sense which could be mediated with human beings" (Bloch 1986: 232-233). Bloch's distinction between capacity and potentiality is the basis of the category of "mere possibility."

Mere vs. real possibilities

To recap, the "fact-based possible" is composed of an internal dimension, an active *capacity* to alter external conditions, and an external dimension, changeable social and/or environmental conditions that Bloch calls *potentialities*. Bloch's distinction between capacity and potentiality permits a categorization of possibilities that remain latent or wither away. For example:

> a blossom can of course let the fruit ripen within it with complete internal conditionality, but if the complete external condition of good weather is missing, then the fruit is still merely possible. Conversely, an even more reductive effect than the missing external condition is produced by the weakness of internal conditions when there is a simultaneous abundance of external ones. (Bloch 1986: 231)

Bloch's (1986: 231-232) social-political example is more illuminating here:

> [o]f course, humanity always sets itself tasks it can solve, but if the great moment for solution is met by a faint-hearted generation, then more than ever this solution is merely possible, i.e., only remains weakly possible. The lack of revolutionary consequences that followed from the 9th November 1918 in Germany provides an example of this.

In this example, Germany failed to bring about a socialist revolution despite ripe conditions, in Bloch's estimation, because the "generation" was too "faint-hearted" or lacked revolutionary consciousness and will (capacity) (see also Haffner 2013). Notably, Bloch uses the term "merely possible" to describe both a capacity that has insufficient or absent potentiality (a fruit-bearing flower without fitting environmental conditions) and a potentiality that has insufficient or absent capacity (the failure of the German left to establish a viable socialist republic despite conducive conditions).

Mere possibility can be contrasted with the "objectively-real Possible," or just "real possibility," the fourth layer of possibility in Bloch's typology. Real possibility is a "future-laden definitiveness in the real itself" (Bloch 1986: 235) or a "future-laden determination" that is "starting to be" and "already underway" (Hudson 1982: 134). Real possibilities differ from the other layers of the possible described above because they are the "materialized" and "contingent manifestations of possibility" that "emerge from the active transformation of the subjective and objective conditions which occurs when they are brought into encounter with one another in practice" (Amsler 2015: 108). Like the fact-based possible external and internal dimensions, real possibilities also have two "sides": (1) an objective realm of "strict determinations which cannot be skipped over," a "What-Is according to possibility," and (2) a forward-looking "unexhausted fullness of expectation," a "What-Is in possibility" (Bloch 1986: 208, emphasis removed). "What-Is according to possibility" is examined via the "cold stream" of Marxism: ideology critique and the socio-economic analysis of "condition-exploration" (e.g., chapters 2 and 1, respectively). "What-Is in possibility" is revealed by Marxism's "warm stream": "prospect exploration," i.e., the exploration of "concrete utopias" already existing in the crevices of the actual (e.g., the second half of this book). Both currents should flow together because the "science of conditions" is necessary to find "the path" (cold stream) and the warm stream of "liberating intention" is needed to illuminate "the goal" and "appeal to the debased, enslaved, abandoned, belittled human being" (Bloch 1986: 209, 1355ff; see Marx 1963: 52).

Unfortunately, unlike the helpful category of the "fact-based possible," Bloch's conception of real possibility is too vague and inclusive (Hudson 1982: 135f). For example, matter is said to be the real possibility of any form that it can deliver throughout its "process" and he believes that we see real possibilities reflected in everything from wishful images to utopian ideas. In Bloch, real possibility is often an underlying propensity driving toward communism or the human being itself: "man is the real possibility of everything which has become of him in his history and, above all, which can still become of him if his progress is not blocked" (Bloch 1986: 235; see also 1968). If the category is to be of much use for us here, a more restricted conception is necessary. Levy's (1997: 178) conceptualization is especially helpful:

> real possibilities ... exhibit a practical relation to the future. They are concretely linked to the hoped-for utopia. In this case utopia is no empty, merely theoretical, possibility, but a very real one. As such it is not only edifying and convincing, but – this is the crux of the matter – it also displays the ways and means for its realization. Utopia is a striving toward the 'real possible,' since present reality already contains the elements for its possible future changes (i.e. possibilities that do not exist *in actu* but are at hand in potential). Humanity's creative capacities which are still dormant can be aroused and realized; this is implied in the idea of utopia.

If real possibility "displays the ways and means for its [utopia's] realization" (Levy 1997: 178) and is "already underway" (Hudson 1982: 134) then mere possibility only dimly illuminates a possible but often unlikely future that is blocked by either a lack of potential (e.g., social organization, technology) or capacity (the right will or revolutionary consciousness). Mere possibility is possibility-in-itself while real possibility is possibility-for-itself.

The early Frankfurt School described a social condition in which the *capacity* for change evaporated, despite the *potentiality* for change, or, more precisely, a condition in which the capacity for change evaporated *due to* the social process that made the potentiality for change possible (see chapter 3). However, owing to a lack of analytical precision, the Frankfurt School's position runs into contradictions when the category of possibility is at hand. *One-Dimensional Man* is an illustrative example of the need for a more robust conceptualization of possibility. On the one hand, Marcuse (1964: 1, 220) uses the term "real possibility" to refer to conditions that make "freedom from want" possible, in contrast to a past "state of lower productivity," suggesting that "real possibility" refers to forces of production that are fettered by current social relations, an aspect of Bloch's notion of *potentiality*. However, in the same work, he argues that any future "transcendent project must be in accordance with the real possibilities open at the attained level of the material and intellectual culture" (Marcuse 1964: 220). The inclusion of real possibilities stemming from already attained developments in "intellectual culture" suggests that the category has a broader meaning than fettered productive forces. The same conceptual paradox appears in later and more hopeful works, where Marcuse continues to speak of the "real possibility for a free society" (1969: 60) though maintains that these "real possibilities of establishing a free society" are obscured (1972: 31).

What eludes the concept of "real possibility" is brought to light by "mere possibility": a condition in which some necessary potentialities (e.g., technological development) and/or capacities (e.g., a vague dissatisfaction with the status quo) exist for a desirable alternative future yet other potentialities (usually a lack of social organization) and/or capacities (usually a lack of revolutionary consciousness) necessary for realizing alternative futures are underdeveloped or absent. The distinction between capacity and potentiality also clarifies the threat ecological degradation and projections of catastrophic climate change pose to dialectical thought: once-possible futures vanish when the external conditions (potentialities) necessary to realize capacities (e.g., the revolutionary will to build a utopia) are irreversibly damaged.

Mere possibilities for a less bad future

In line with negative dialectics, and unlike the detection of real possibilities, the category of mere possibility does not allow for outlining clear pathways for realizing desirable alternative social futures, let alone coherent blueprints, usually due to the lack of a historical subject and, now, the likelihood of an unsavable future. At the same time, unlike a purely negative dialectics, recognizing the merely possible clears space for a form of affirmative or positive speculation that negative dialectics often avoids: "a copy of what the object can hypothetically become through variability and inter-relation" (Hudson 1982: 133). In other words, distinguishing between capacity and potentiality, and assuming that possibility is not synonymous with real possibility, delivers a warmer negative dialectics, already present in some of Adorno's work, that not only indirectly and negatively illuminates the possible, like the Frankfurt School, but can also point to concrete political alternatives, even if these alternatives remain merely possible alternatives.

The category of mere possibility has two practical implications for negative dialectics. First, drawing attention to mere possibilities can highlight the existence of alternatives that, while blocked or constrained in the present, may become real possibilities in the future. The assumption is that drawing attention to these partially formed and constrained alternatives increases the chances or probability that they can be actualized when the "doors" to a better future are no longer "barricaded" (Adorno 1991: 173). However, as negative dialectics emphasizes, this reasonable—reasonable because it is rooted in partially formed potentiality or capacity—and hopeful anticipation does *not* mean actualization is predetermined. Any warmer negative dialectics should continue to consciously avoid assumptions about teleological inevitability.

The second practical implication of the category of mere possibility for negative dialectics is allowing critique to stay true to its origins and ethical thrust: "changing the concrete conditions under which men suffer," as Horkheimer (1972: 32) plainly put it. In a society that still lacks the real possibility for change due to the absence of a revolutionary subject, negative dialectics follows Horkheimer's (1978: 237) late reformulation of critical theory's commitment: "[i]f one wishes to define the good as the attempt to abolish evil, it can be determined. And this is the teaching of Critical Theory. But the opposite—to define evil by the good—would be an impossibility, even in morality." However, there are periods and events that are so dire and catastrophic that they compel the dialectic to propose concrete solutions, even if these solutions are constrained, inadequate to the task, barely-formed, and unlikely to actualize. Climate change is a case in point.

Merely possible climate change solutions

This section brings the concept of mere possibility to bear on the social and political-economic dimensions of climate politics. It was due to the inadequacy and ineffectiveness of current climate change strategies that co-authors and I (Stuart et al. 2020a) sought to identify "transitional" climate change mitigation strategies that:

- Have the potential to increase social wellbeing in a just manner while effectively decreasing carbon emissions.
- Already exist in pockets of the existing order "but as present only intermittently, partially, or potentially" (Young 2001: 10).

- Can possibly overcome a major driver of climate change, which we formulate as a contradiction between capital's need to expand production, on the one hand, and the destructive effects expansionistic production has on the climate system, on the other (the "capital-climate contradiction" discussed in chapter 1).

The following climate change responses were identified as genuine "win-win" strategies for the climate and society as well as having the potential to help transcend the capital-climate contradiction:

- Socializing energy systems, such as community energy projects (e.g., Kunze and Becker 2015; Gunderson et al. 2018) and proposals to nationalize-and-shrink fossil fuel industries (e.g., Gowan 2018a).
- Work time reduction (e.g., Schor 2005; Rosnick and Weisbrot 2006; Knight et al. 2013; Rosnick 2013; Pullinge 2014; Fitzgerald et al. 2015).
- Economic democracy (e.g., Johanisova and Wolf 2012).
- Democratizing global climate governance (e.g., Dryzek and Stevenson 2011).

These strategies have the *potential* to significantly reduce total carbon emissions if they took hold as prominent climate mitigation strategies.

While Stuart et al. (2020a) deliver an integrative analysis that cannot be reproduced here, I briefly summarize one example: work time reduction. Shorter working hours are associated with significant reductions in environmental pressure and resource use (e.g., Rosnick and Weisbrot 2006; Knight et al. 2013; Fitzgerald et al. 2015). For example, among OECD countries, those with shorter working hours have significantly lower carbon emissions and ecological footprints (Knight et al. 2013).

If the US used productivity gains to shorten the workweek or extend vacation time, as opposed to producing more, then the country would consume around 20 percent less energy (Rosnick and Weisbrot 2006) and, at a global level, if working hours were reduced 0.5 percent annually for the next century, it would "eliminate about one-quarter to one-half, if not more, of any warming that is not already locked in" (Rosnick 2013: 124).

Despite the potential of work time reduction and the other climate mitigation strategies listed above, there are at least three interrelated reasons to be skeptical of the likelihood of the wide and effective adoption of the above strategies: (1) most political trends will hinder rather than realize merely possible climate change solutions; (2) the lack of a social movement to implement these mitigation strategies at the scale and pace necessary to meet climate targets; and (3) the threat of cooptation if they are not pursued as a collective-political project. In the case of work time reduction, the social organizations historically responsible for reductions in working hours, labor unions, were coopted in the US into bargaining for higher levels of material consumption instead of work time reduction (Obach 2004: 344) and there has been a steep decline in labor's power in many advanced industrial societies, especially since the late 1970s, for a number of structural reasons, including global economic liberalization, financialization of the economy, "flexible" labor markets, a rightward political shift, outdated organizing methods, demographic changes, deindustrialization, and anti-labor practices and legislation (e.g., Bryson et al. 2011). In other words, these strategies have the *technical potentiality* to significantly contribute to climate change mitigation yet are constrained, though not fully blocked, by social-structural conditions (i.e., a lack of *social potentiality*) as well as by the lack of radical consciousness and collective will (*capacity*). In a word, they are *mere* possibilities, not real possibilities.

Identifying what is merely possible in climate politics

is not only a useful descriptive concept. More importantly, it helps evade three problematic tendencies in prescriptive assessments of climate politics discussed in chapters 2 and 3: green growth, ecological revolution, and climate fatalism. First, the category of possibility in general helps circumvent the most common yet most deceptive tendency in climate political analysis: repeating naïve techno-optimistic and market-friendly talking points about "green growth," "green capitalism," "ecological modernization," etc. even though the strategies associated with these frames have had limited success and unintended, counterintuitive impacts. In contrast, the very concept of possibility in social analysis directs attention to what is not normative or fully emerged. Striving to locate social alternatives within the real is central to any dialectical analysis of society. Directed by the concept of mere possibility, such an approach allows for a prescriptive analysis of climate change to look beyond mainstream approaches that are known to be ineffective.

The category of mere possibility also assists in modifying the reasonable case for an ecological revolution (e.g., Foster 2009; Magdoff and Williams 2017). At this time, there does not seem to be a historical subject that will carry out the revolution (see chapter 3). While there are seeds of resistance and unrest—from the Yellow Vests in France to the recent eruption of protests in Ecuador, Lebanon, and the US—it is difficult to see these seeds growing into an international movement with the power, organization, and vision necessary to replace global capitalism with an ecological society. Both capacity (revolutionary consciousness) and social potentiality (sufficient organization and political infrastructure) are absent. Even in the exceedingly unlikely case of the emergence of a revolutionary movement that overcame the many failings of past revolutionary strategies (see Wright 2010), one barricade to revolutionary transformation cannot be assumed away, especially in the US in the age of surveillance capitalism: the astounding power of "the repressive state apparatus" — the government, military, courts, police, and prison system (Althusser 1971) —, forces which would strive to squash, and likely succeed in squashing, any revolutionary movement. While I do not dispute the argument that fundamental social and economic changes are necessary to avoid catastrophic climate change, a revolution is highly unlikely, at least in the near future.

The third problematic tendency that the category of mere possibility circumvents is climate fatalism. On the one hand, I think pessimism, so long as it does not become its own form of alienated reconciliation (see chapter 6), is an appropriate starting point for the situation and even necessary to resist a climate change discourse and politics that is packed full of "fraudulent hope" (Bloch 1986). Although Bloch opposed the Frankfurt School's pessimism (see Tar 1977: 206), even he, a defender of "militant optimism," argues that pessimism, as long as it is not made absolute, is a "better traveling companion than cheap credulity" and "constitutes the critical coldness of Marxism" (Bloch 1986: 199; see also Levitas and Sargisson 2003). However, the catastrophic stakes of climate change still oblige the dialectician to report imperfect and unclear paths forward. In the same way that the horror of the Holocaust compelled the master of negative dialectics — a method that shuns cheap, programmatic solutions — to propose an imperfect affirmative prescription, the stakes of climate change compel us to do the same today. This does not mean that dialectical thought should give up ideology critique and political-economic analysis in favor of empty promises. The "cold stream" of Marxist analysis should remain central. Instead, it means that the direness of particular events and eras warrant deficient "prospect exploration" contextualized with negative findings.

Mundane transcendence: Everyday illuminations of a less bad future

Along with identifying merely possible alternative social futures, experiences of mundane transcendence can also keep dialectical thought from drowning under the waves of regression and barbarism. Karen Ng (2015: 395) defines Honneth's notion of "intramundane transcendence" as "an experience in which the normative interest in emancipation can still get a foothold — *within* existing social reality." For example, there is the rational potential of communicative action immanent in the interactions of speaking and acting subjects in Habermas (1987). In Marcuse (1955), there are life-affirming drives that seek to overcome social restraints. In Adorno (1984), there is negative potential of bleak modernist art. Even in the defeatist and exceedingly pessimistic late Horkheimer, there is still the longing for "the totally other" as a secularized theological basis for critique (Ott 2006).

I modify the term to "mundane transcendence" to underscore the everydayness and apparent unremarkableness of these experiences in comparison to the usual Marxist method of searching for a better future in fettered productive forces, social-political organization, and revolutionary consciousness. The latter method is sustained with the help of the concept of mere possibility. Mundane transcendence, in comparison, is the hope that fuels dialectical thought in everyday life. It is not the belief that there is a "sign of a transcendent presence" when "life shows some similarity to life, for once," as opposed to the capitalist norm, where life is "kept going only for production's and consumption's sake" (Adorno 1973a: 376). Instead, mundane transcendence is a hope that the possibility of the transcendent, soon a catastrophic yet still livable future, has not completely vanished. The first volume of Bloch's *Principle of Hope* is a poetic encyclopedia of mundane transcendences. From the play of children and daydreaming to the feelings of adolescents in love and an old man's "wish and ability to be without vulgar haste, to see what is important, to forget what is unimportant" (Bloch 1986: 41), mundane transcendence is central to Bloch's analysis and worldview, where being is always becoming, searching, and wishing, and thinking is always a "venturing beyond."

Mundane transcendence sets itself apart from alienated reconciliation to the extent that it inspires hope for a less bad *future* in a way that does not encourage a passive acceptance of the present status quo. To provide a couple of examples before expanding upon a longer illustration:

- Studying history to find that past societies have been organized in qualitatively distinct ways, so differently that it is impossible to explain economic relations with modern frameworks of understanding (e.g., Mauss 1967). These past realities denaturalize contemporary social relations. In such cases, Benjamin's advice to root historical materialism in the past is well-founded (see chapter 4).
- Witnessing or experiencing genuine love and care. These tender exceptions to typical forms of manipulation, rushed scripted interactions, and outright exploitation demonstrate that human activity has not been wholly reduced to domination and instrumentality and, therefore, there are still signs that social relations could be humanized. Zygmunt Bauman (2003: 70) is right, for now, that "[t]he need for solidarity seems to withstand and survive market assaults."

Mundane transcendence, as reconciliation with the possibility of a less bad future, positions thinking in opposition to the current social order. However, this concept ought to be used carefully, mindful of the way that social-structural forces colonize experiences of mundane transcendence, lest critical theory itself becomes "domesticated" (conformist) and "idealist" (i.e., wrongly believing that these experiences sit outside power structures) (Thompson 2016). Experiences of mundane transcendence too easily morph into forms of alienated reconciliation. For example, the realization that the past is qualitatively different from the present can either inspire the hope for a new form of human society to emerge in the future (anticipatory reconciliation) or can inspire a fatalistic romanticism, a fatalism that reconciles consciousness with a reality that cannot be changed because a Golden Age cannot be restored (alienated reconciliation). Or take the experience of compassion, which can, on the one hand, kindle solidarity with others to build a society in which the systemic causes of suffering are addressed (anticipatory reconciliation) (Horkheimer 1993a), or, far more often, inspire charitable actions or campaigns that ignore and, therefore, reproduce the social-structural basis of widespread suffering (alienated reconciliation) (Mussell 2013: 62).

Commodification is the easiest way to defang mundane transcendence. For example, read through the eyes of an advertiser, Bloch's *Philosophy of Hope* is a textbook of human desires just waiting to be tapped by the market. He knew how easy it is to recuperate dreams and wishes with commodities as well as fashion new alienated needs.

Most people in the street look as if they are thinking about something else entirely. The something else is predominantly money, but also what it could be changed into. Otherwise it would not be so easy to lure with jewellery, to attract with a beautiful figure. ... In this way the shopping street is also steeped in dreams ... A woman stands in front of the shop-window, looking at lizard-skin shoes trimmed with chamois leather, a man goes past, looks at the woman, and so both of them have a share of the wishful land. There is enough happiness in the world, only not for me: the wish tells itself this, wherever it goes. (Bloch 1986: 33)

Despite the ease by which mundane transcendence can slip from an anticipatory to an alienated form of reconciliation, it is still an essential foundation of dialectical thought, and can inform the search for a less bad dystopia. The following subsection provides a more detailed example of mundane transcendence related to the goal of a damaged reconciliation with nature: the insight that animals at rest or "living in the moment" can teach us how to live a better life.

An illustration of mundane transcendence: Learning about the good life from animals

As discussed in chapter 4, Adorno argues that what is considered progress in civilization is the blind domination of nature and that a genuine realization of progress, which he defines as the avoidance of catastrophe, would require the end of what is conventionally considered progress. The end of progress means the harmonization of human-nature relations as well as human reason and human nature, two interrelated goals termed "reconciliation." This section discusses how this vision was partly inspired by observing, or perhaps imagining or remembering, animals at rest—a feat of mundane transcendence.

The thought that humans can learn from the wisdom of animals is a common motif in a marginal philosophical tradition: pessimism. Sometimes this argument is made negatively, when asserting that humans are "diseased animals" due to the capacities for self-consciousness and the abstract awareness of time (Unamuno 1972). At other times, there are overt arguments that humans should learn from, or at least envy, animals, especially when at rest, due to their "calm and undisturbed enjoyment of the present moment" (Schopenhauer 1974: 296).

Similarly, Eduard von Hartmann (1931, vol. 3: 76) comments that:

> the brutes are happier (i.e., less miserable) than man, because the excess of pain which an animal has to bear is less than that which a man has to bear. Only think how comfortably an ox or a pig lives, almost as if it had learned from Aristotle to seek freedom from care and sorrow, instead (like man) of hunting after happiness.

Cioran (1973: 193) complains that humanity has "rebelled" against the "divine" state of inactivity and, due to our busyness and constantly renewed desire for the new, man shows himself "unworthy of his ancestor: the need for novelty is the characteristic of an alienated gorilla."

The Frankfurt School's admiration of the animal's comfort in idleness is formulated differently from the Schopenhauerian lessons drawn by pessimists. Instead of naturalizing human busyness as inevitable or recommending individual renunciation, forms of alienated reconciliation, the Frankfurt School's admiration for animals at rest is projected into the future as a utopian image, a goal to faintly direct the dialectic. For Adorno and Horkheimer, remembering human animality, while maintaining and heightening the constructive aspects of human reason, was an essential step in the process of reconciliation. They believe that animals can "teach" human beings about the good life. During a conversation, the authors of *Dialectic of Enlightenment* deemed animal life as representative of the goals of happiness and freedom.

> Horkheimer: "Happiness would be an animal condition viewed from the perspective of whatever has ceased to be animal [i.e. human reason]."

Adorno: "Animals could teach us what happiness is."

Horkheimer: "To achieve the condition of an animal at the level of reflection—that is freedom." (Adorno and Horkheimer 2011: 16)

Inverting over two-thousand years of Western rationalism, though defenders of reason, Horkheimer and Adorno believe that animality is something to be *regained* and *preserved* in the unfolding of reason, rather than something to be overcome.

The theme of humanity critically coming to terms with its own animality to achieve reconciliation is clearest in one of the most striking brief essays in Adorno's (1978: 155-57) *Minima Moralia*, "*Sur l'Eau*," where he portrays a reconciled socialist human being as a docile and contemplative animal. Despite being a short reflection, the content of "*Sur l'Eau*" has been discussed at length by others with sometimes contradictory interpretations (Jameson 2005: 172ff; Chrostowska 2013: 108ff; Marwood 2016). It "occupies a *privileged* place in an understanding of his oeuvre," as Marwood (2016: 834) put it, though I disagree with the latter's reading (see below). I present the core themes of "*Sur l'Eau*" in two steps. The first concerns Adorno's criticism of the idea of communism as one of endless production and activity, and the second, an alternative vision of utopia as peaceful rest.

Adorno (1978: 155-156) opens "*Sur l'Eau*" with the following:

[h]e who asks what is the goal of an emancipated society is given answers such as the fulfilment of human possibilities or the richness of life. ... There is tenderness only in the coarsest demand: that no-one shall go hungry any more. ... Into the wishful image of an uninhibited, vital, creative man has seeped the very fetishism of commodities which in bourgeois society brings with it inhibition, impotence, the sterility of the never-changing. ... The naïve supposition of

an unambiguous development towards increased production is itself a piece of that bourgeois outlook which permits development in only one direction because, integrated into a totality, dominated by quantification, it is hostile to qualitative difference.

Here we find an early socialist critique of the socialist brand of "productivism," or the goal of using "unfettered" productive forces for *more* production for the sake of production, a normative aim common in turn of the twentieth century socialisms, though a vision that still lingers today, even among alleged "eco-socialists" (for critiques, see Foster 2017; Kallis 2019). Adorno rightly claims this image of an emancipated society is merely an extension of, rather than alternative to, the "unfettered activity" and "freedom as frantic bustle" characteristic of capitalism (Adorno 1978: 156).

Following, he offers an alternative image of utopia to those promoted by socialist productivism:

[i]f we imagine emancipated society as emancipation from precisely such totality, then vanishing-lines come into view that have little in common with increased production and its human reflections. ... [A] society rid of its fetters might take thought that even the forces of production are not the deepest substratum of man, but represent his historical form adapted to the production of commodities. Perhaps the true society will grow tired of development and, out of freedom, leave possibilities unused, instead of storming under a confused compulsion to the conquest of strange stars. A mankind which no longer knows want will begin to have an inkling of the delusory, futile nature of all the arrangements hitherto made in order to escape want, which used wealth to produce want on a larger scale. ... *Rien faire comme une bête* [Doing nothing, like an animal], lying on water and

looking peacefully at the sky, "being, nothing else, without any further definition and fulfilment", might take the place of process, act, satisfaction, and so truly keep the promise of dialectical logic that it would culminate in its origin. None of the abstract concepts comes closer to fulfilled utopia than that of eternal peace. (Adorno 1978: 156-157)

This second quoted portion above anticipates that a good society would *not* strive to actualize all potentialities or seek to discover previously unexplored environments. Instead, we are invited to envision utopia as restful peace: a reconciled human-animal on a boat "'being, nothing else, without any further definition and fulfilment'." Although uncited, the author assumes the latter quote is from Hegel's (2010: 59) description of being in the first tripartite (Being-Nothing-Becoming) in the *Science of Logic*, which would account for the expectation for the dialectic to keep its "promise" to "culminate in its origin" (i.e., Being). This vision of utopia as quiescent passivity can be contrasted with both the conception of "freedom as frantic bustle" of capitalist societies, which uses "wealth to produce want on a larger scale" (Adorno 1978: 156, 157), as well as the productivist anticipation of unfettered development of the productive forces in a communist society.

In addition to Hegel's description of being, there are a handful of other direct yet implicit intellectual influences and references to other works in the short essay, which further shine light on its significance and meaning. The title of the short essay ("*Sur l'Eau*" [at sea, adrift, on the river]) is likely a reference to Guy de Maupassant's 1881 short story, "*Sur l'Eau*," not his 1888 book by the same name (see Marwood 2016: 836ff). In the short story, a boatman finds himself stuck in the middle of a river, panicking due to incoming fog. After the fog dissipates the boatman takes in and appreciates the natural beauty of the river's ecology at night as a fellow animal, as one of "'[*des*] *bêtes de l'eau*' ('the beasts of the water')" (quoted in Marwood 2016: 837). While helping the boatman free his boat in the morning, a fisherman finds that the anchor was caught on a dead woman's body, likely a suicide judging by the large stone tied around her neck. I disagree with Marwood's (2016: 839) interpretation that this literary reference means that the passage is another instance in which Adorno shows that "positive utopia is revealed to be just another discreet dream of the bourgeoisie." Instead, I think it is meant to qualify the utopian image by reminding us that if any decent society is ever formed out of the "nightmare of human history" (Jameson 2005: 74) it will be scarred by this history of violence and suffering, which should never be rationalized or justified. As discussed in chapter 4, opposition to theodicy is a common Frankfurt School motif.

There are other possible literary and philosophical inspirations for the passage, such as Proust's description of Vivonne River in *Swann's Way* (Peters 2014: 198) and Rousseau's (1992: 62-73) reflections on the happiness and self-contentment he experienced when lying on a boat during a short, relaxing vacation at St. Peter Island in western Switzerland (Thomä 2012: 124; Chrostowska 2013: 110ff). Regardless of the intellectual inspiration, the important point here is it is an experience of mundane transcendence, a utopian wish built from material "*within* existing social reality" (Ng 2015: 395), a scene meant to help envision a "true society." A positive utopian image is a rare instance in Adorno's work, which is almost unwavering in the conviction that positive utopianism will betray or "sabotage" the possibility of utopia (Adorno 1991: 175; Chrostowska 2013: 99ff, 108f). Indeed, in Adorno, reconciliation as a concept "stands in an aporetic relationship to the unreconciled world that we live in and thus can be neither conceptualized nor represented" (Allen 2016: 169). In the above fragment, however, he evokes the human-animal image to deliver a "glimpse" into a "utopia achieved" (Chrostowska 2013: 108).

I use the Frankfurt School's belief that a liberated human society can learn from animals at rest as the extended illustration of mundane transcendence because this utopian image resonates with calls to reduce carbon emissions through less work and more low-impact leisure (Gunderson 2018). A "true society," according to Adorno, would not only work less, but use our time away from work in qualitatively different ways than we do now. "Free time" today means little more than consuming the many administered treats and games offered by the culture industry to cure us of the boredom attached to unfreedom and unimaginativeness required in an instrumentally rational society (Adorno 1998: 167-175). In contrast, Adorno's reconciled socialist human-animal preserves the capacity for reflection yet casts off the hysterical busyness that characterizes modern life in capitalist societies as well as challenges the orthodox anti-ecological conception of a communist society as one of endless growth and development.

I also use *"Sur l'Eau"* as an extended illustration because it demonstrates how to resist experiences of mundane transcendence from slipping from anticipatory longing to alienated reconciliation. Unlike the pessimists who admire animals in order to naturalize the "diseased" consciousness of humans or to promote individual renunciation, the Frankfurt School's reflections on animal inactivity—because they project restful peace into the future as a goal to be attained—have political implications and position thinking against present conditions. Attaining a state of rest would require qualitative changes in the social order that structurally requires the subjugation of life to production and consumption. Indeed, peace is the absolute aim of the "genuine utopian."

The final will is that to be truly present. So that the lived moment belongs to us and we to it and 'Stay awhile' could be said to it. Man wants at last to enter into the Here and Now as himself, wants to enter his full life without postponement and distance. The genuine utopian will is definitely not endless striving, rather: it wants to see the merely immediate and thus so unpossessed nature of self-location and being-here finally mediated, illuminated and fulfilled, fulfilled happily and adequately. (Bloch 1986: 16)

However, before one gets lost in the *wish* for peace, a lostness that can become its own form of alienated reconciliation by, for example, finding solace in mindfulness classes, we must keep one foot in the present and build a movement to socially achieve peace.

Conclusion: All is not lost

Despite the likelihood of a catastrophic future, two forms of anticipatory reconciliation are still accessible in nonideal conditions: mere possibility and mundane transcendence. Mere possibilities refer to alternative social futures partially formed in the present yet lack either objective or subjective dimensions to actualize. Most often, mere possibilities are *technical potentialities* that lack either social and political organization ("social potentiality") or revolutionary consciousness ("capacity"). The notion of mere possibility helps negative dialectics face a grim reality head on yet loosens the prohibition against naming alternatives latent in already existing conditions that could be tapped and expanded for a less bad world. Mundane transcendence refers to everyday experiences—from genuine kindness to observing animals at rest—that inspire hope and remind us that a less bad future is possible, that all is not lost. Due to objective conditions described in chapters 3 and 4, both forms of anticipatory reconciliation lack the certainty and confidence of past developments of dialectical thought. However, because they point to the possibility of a less bad future, they provide foundations for critique and keep dialectics on life support in dark times.

The always-nagging practical questions without clear answers remain: (1) How do we build a movement for a less bad future? (2) If a successful movement is highly unlikely in the foreseeable future, what may we hope for? The following and final chapter addresses both questions.

Chapter 6

Hope in Negativity: Revolutionary Reformism Without Optimism

Until all are fed and have a seat at the table

Hope is the fuel of dialectical thinking, an anticipatory consciousness that is still tenable so long as its yearning is reformulated to account for the real material undermining of potentiality due to the ecological crisis and the unlikelihood of radical social change in the foreseeable future. Terry Eagleton's (2015) defense of "hope without optimism" is pertinent in an age in which "progress" is degrading the possibility of saving the future. So is Christopher Lasch's (1991: 39) awareness that hope lives on today, not through optimism, but through "darker voices":

> [i]t is the darker voices especially that speak to us now, not because they speak in tones of despair but because they help us distinguish "optimism" from hope and thus give us the courage to confront the mounting difficulties that threaten to overwhelm us.

When we are doomed on all fronts, "negativity" in the Hegelian-Marxian sense of non-affirmative, oppositional, or defiant thinking is closely bound to the common-sense meaning of "negative" as pessimistic or despairing. Indeed, this association is already present in Hegel (Marasco 2015). In her analysis of the "dialectical passion" of despair in Adorno and others, Robyn Marasco (2015: 5) puts it this way: "[d]espair can never fully let go of its familiar and estranged other [hope]." Despair is not hope's executioner. One often despairs because one

145

hopes and hopes because one despairs. The real undertaker of hope is alienated reconciliation, the preemptive consolation of consciousness with the way things are. In contrast, the dialectic is the self-responsibility of the slave to remain restless and "think beyond" the established order of things until all are fed and have a seat at the table. The dark side of this ethic of restlessness is put beautifully in another famous passage from the preface of the *Phenomenology*:

> [t]he life of the mind is not one that shuns death, and keeps clear of destruction; it endures death and in death maintains its being. It only wins to its truth when it finds itself utterly torn asunder. It is this mighty power, not by being a positive which turns away from the negative ... [O]n the contrary, mind is this power only by looking the negative in the face, and dwelling with it. (Hegel 1967: 93)

The hope of the dialectic today is for a less bad future disciplined by the recognition that things very well may change for the worse, a hope captured in Gramsci's (1971: 175n) oft-quoted reflection in prison, advising Marxists to have a "[p]essimism of the intelligence" and an "optimism of the will."

This brief concluding chapter addresses two questions that infect the mind of every radical who walks the tightrope above a crevasse of fatalism while peering into a future already in flames. First, how can we build a successful socialist movement? Second, how can we preserve hope if we continue to fail, which seems likely in the foreseeable future? To the first question, I reply that "revolutionary reformism"—roughly, strong social-democratic reforms intended to spur a transition to democratic socialism—is, despite its pitfalls, the only relatively viable first step for building a radical politics today. To the second, I argue that even if the dialectic is in bed with pessimism, it remains a hopeful and non-fatalistic partner.

First steps for realizing mere possibilities: Revolutionary reformism

As discussed in previous chapters, the likelihood of catastrophic climate change is not the only challenge for building a socialist movement today. Predating climate change projections was the problem of the vanishing revolutionary subject. How do we foster a socialist politics without a clear historical subject? This does not mean that class politics is irrelevant. Far from it. It means that the working class is still only a class-in-itself, not yet a class-for-itself with the organization and will to abolish itself along with class relations. In such conditions, how do we create a socialist politics?

I agree with others that the first step to building support for a socialist transition is large-scale social-democratic reforms whose long-term goal is to move beyond social democracy toward democratic socialism (for popular accounts, see Robinson 2019; Sunkara 2019). This path of "non-reformist reforms" (Gorz 1967) or "symbiotic" transformation (Wright 2010) has been termed "revolutionary reformism" (Miliband et al. 1985/1986; see also Goldmann in Cohen 1994: 266ff) and, more recently, "class struggle social democracy" (Sunkara 2019) won through a combination of grassroots organizing and "class struggle campaigns" (Uetricht and Day 2020). Robinson (2019: ch. 8) lays out and defends a laundry list of achievable agendas in the US to nourish a budding social-democratic movement, including Medicare for All, ending private prisons, increasing federal funding for states who reduce tuition costs, paid family and medical leave, introducing a universal childcare program, making voting easier, expanding the supreme court and introducing term limits, implementing ranked-choice voting, introducing a more progressive tax code, and making sure the rich pay their taxes.

In the context of climate change, non-reformist reforms are compatible with an uncastrated Green New Deal. Take Senator

Sanders' (n.d.) Green New Deal plan, which, despite blind spots, includes proposals to:

- "Transform our energy system away from fossil fuels to 100 percent energy efficiency and sustainable energy by 2030 at the latest...
- "Ensure a just transition for energy workers...
- "Build the 7.4 million affordable housing units to close the affordable housing gap across the country and guarantee safe, decent, accessible affordable housing.
- "Build public transit that is affordable, accessible, fast, and resilient...
- "Incentivize farmers to develop ecologically regenerative farming systems that sharply reduce emissions; sequester carbon; and heal our soils, forests, and prairie lands."

These proposals and others like them, many of which are publicly popular (Data for Progress n.d.), would not only increase human wellbeing while decreasing emissions, but could also lay some of the foundations for a movement and vision to transition out of capitalism.

A renewed socialist movement is dependent on increasing the wellbeing of the common person (Wright 2010) and, in the near future, it is difficult to imagine any other institution to do this than the state, one kept in check by broad-based progressive movements. Starting with state-instituted social-democratic reforms will concretely demonstrate to people that life need not be so precarious and unfulfilling. Because concrete improvements in wellbeing will breathe life back into the utopian spirit in an era in which it is "easier to imagine the end of the world than to imagine the end of capitalism" (Jameson 2003: 73; cf. Fisher 2009), life-saving and -improving reforms are the best first step to heightening mere possibilities for a less bad future into real possibilities.

The promotion of "revolutionary reformism" beginning with social-democratic reforms is never free from qualifiers. Some of the most important qualifiers include (1) a need to avoid increasing total energy and material throughput and (2) ensuring that "revolutionary reformism" does not, once again, mutate into status quo maintenance à la liberal-centrist reformism. First, a radical social-democratic transition must avoid relying on economic growth as an unjustifiable stand-in for increasing human wellbeing. Economic growth that goes beyond satisfying basic needs does not lead to increases in happiness (for review, see Sekulova 2015) and does not seem to increase human wellbeing per unit of environmental pressure after a certain level of affluence (Dietz et al. 2012). Further, increasing overall economic growth is associated with increases in carbon emissions and it is unlikely that unlimited "green growth" is possible (see chapter 2). Any renewed socialist movement must abandon the "Promethean" and "Cornucopian" social imaginaries that not only characterize capitalism, but also some socialist visions. The merely possible climate change solutions summarized in chapter 5 were selected with awareness of the need for overall "degrowth" in wealthy countries (see Stuart et al. 2020a). Work time reduction in particular should return as a defining and realizable goal of a renewed leftist politics.

A second long-known limitation of social democracy relates to the welfare state's structural tendency to side with capitalist interests when any effort is made to move beyond social democracy. When push comes to shove, the social-democratic state supports capital accumulation above all else because, among other reasons, the electorate still depends on the success of capitalist firms and, if more transformative agendas are pushed — such as Rudolf Meidner's plan to transfer the ownership of firms to workers at the height of Swedish social democracy (Gowan 2018b) —, capital fights back (McCarthy 2018). Avoiding this trap in a renewed social democracy requires the push of a large socialist movement, whose existence, though, depends on demonstrating that life-changing reforms are possible at all. This is especially true in the US, where even the smallest crumbs gained during the Keynesian-Fordist era have been snatched up through neoliberal reforms. The socialist magazine *Jacobin* publishes readable and helpful writings on the tensions of supporting social democracy in the short-term while holding longer-term transitional aspirations (e.g., Frase 2016; Gowan 2017; Schwartz and Sunkara 2017; McCarthy 2018). The goal is not to replace "subversive and visionary" measures with so called "reasonable" measures, because the latter, as Jacoby (1999: 25) shows, are almost always implicit justifications for the status quo with minor market or cultural reforms. Instead, the goal is to show that wellbeing-increasing social programs are possible and achievable. Improving livelihood empowers people to see that a less bad future is possible.

Revolutionaries will reply that left-reformist electoral political campaigns, even when successful, are quickly disciplined by the systemic imperatives of existing institutions, with Greece's Syriza hanging in the crowded gallows of left-wing disappointments as a contemporary case study. Further, two recent national-level electoral campaigns that approximate this strategy in the Anglosphere failed: the Jeremy Corbyn campaign in the UK and, even less radical, the Sanders campaign in the US. But the case for a revolutionary-reformist strategy on the left is, at bottom, a process of elimination. The only alternatives seem to be left-wing accelerationism and variations of traditional revolutionary socialisms, visions that, to polemically oversimplify, share at least one common strategy: waiting for the Great Change brought about by the self-transformation of the Historical Subject. While there are many reasons to doubt the emergence and success of revolutionary transformation (e.g., the stranglehold of the culture industry on consciousness), one reason, discussed in chapter 5, is decisive: the ever-expanding power of the repressive state apparatus. The belief that a revolution is even a mere possibility in the US should reflect on the following exact if rhetorical question, and the implications of the negative answer: Is there any imaginable circumstance in which the US military would side with a climate revolution?

We can no longer afford to presuppose the eventual emergence of positive qualitative change, or, what is often the same, assume that things will get better just because they are getting worse, especially in the age of climate change (Stoner and Melathopoulos 2016). As explained in previous chapters, the progressive apocalypticism of past developments of the dialectic are a dead-end when the future is already billowing smoke. The choice for the left in our historical situation is between (1) building a social-democratic movement with ecological and democratic socialism as a horizonal aspiration and (2) "standing on the sidelines screaming ultra-left slogans" (Burgis 2019).

Leaving aside questions about what young people may mean by the word "socialism," there are few data points that give this author more hope for the future than a widely discussed 2015 poll showing that the majority of Americans aged 18 to 29 view socialism favorably (Ekins 2015). Further, although the Sanders campaign and related campaigns failed, this does not mean that the thirst for a different world, especially among young people, vanished with their campaigns (Uetricht and Day 2020). However, we should not assume that a better society will necessarily come to fruition as young people age. Take the trajectory of the young radicals of the 1960s, a period far more revolutionary and organized than our own. Some of the 60s radicals are still fighting the good fight. Indeed, much of this book is influenced by conversations with, and reading the work of, those who are. However, consider the following data points to the ideal type of the 1968er: over 70 percent of Democratic voters aged 65 and older voted for Hillary Clinton over Sanders in the 2016 presidential primaries (Zitner et al. 2016) and overwhelmingly supported Joe Biden over Sanders (e.g., Sachs 2020). Of course, the liberal boomer's preference for neoliberal war hawks who are economically right of Richard Nixon over a social democrat must be understood in a particular historical context: the rise of the relatively autonomous and well-paid professional-managerial class, though a class that increasingly has a more traditional "proletarian character" (Williams 2016). Closing this section with this warning serves as a reminder to exorcise the dialectic of all remnants of assumptions about teleological inevitability and the imminent formation of a historical subject, flagellations that can lead dialectics to despair.

Negation of the negation of the negation etc.: Pessimism and the dialectic

None of the left's continued failures would have surprised the Frankfurt School. Before the Frankfurt School, there were periods in modern history when our disappointed predecessors have questioned and even inverted the modern theory of progress, beliefs hardly confined to the academy or the left. For example, take a strand of German intellectual culture, beginning with Arthur Schopenhauer's fame near the end of his life (1860), followed by the popularity of Eduard von Hartmann's *Philosophy of the Unconscious,* first published in 1868 — a comically dark "nihilistic eschatology," where the telos of the universe, an irrational mistake, is projected to end when humanity collectivity realizes that "all is vanity" (Darnoi 1967) — , passing through a large audience for Nietzsche's life-affirming "Dionysian" pessimism, and culminating in Oswald Spengler's best-selling two volumes of *Decline of the West* in 1918 and 1922. Today, for social reasons described in chapter 1, we experience a similar if less philosophically inclined collective foreboding that this will all end in a disaster. Although there is a mere possibility to change course, and this possibility must be kept in constant gaze, the likelihood of a catastrophic future invites us to revisit more pessimistic theories of history and projections for the future. A dialectical reading allows for a non-fatalistic form of pessimism that acts as a bastion of hope (Adorno 1967b; Gunderson 2015a).

Pessimism has historically referred to a theoretical diagnosis about humanity and its place in the universe composed of common propositions and motifs, including: time is burdensome (time-consciousness illuminates death and impermanence); history is ironic (e.g., advancements in science and technology are inextricably hooked to various great costs); freedom and happiness are antithetical (e.g., reason's illusion-destroying capacity undermines comfortable fictions); and human existence is absurd (Dienstag 2006: 19ff). The prescriptions offered by pessimistic systems typically either recommend some level of resignation, withdrawal, or renunciation, on the one hand, or spontaneous life-affirmation, on the other. The argument for resignation, found in thinkers as diverse as the stoics, Augustine, Calvin, Rousseau, Kant, Cioran, and, most famously, Schopenhauer (1969: Book 4; Peters 2014: ch. 9), is that unruly desires make us miserable, so we ought to minimize them to achieve relative calm and freedom from pain (Dienstag 2006). Nietzsche (1967: 17) condemns this Schopenhauerian "pessimism of weakness" and calls for an alternative "pessimism of strength" that confronts suffering, cruelty, and meaningless with self-affirmation and hardness rather than renunciation and compassion. This "Dionysian" pessimism (Nietzsche 1974: 331) is also found in thinkers like Giacomo Leopardi and Albert Camus (Dienstag 2006).

To ask one to intellectually engage with this tradition, let alone learn lessons from it, is a thorny invitation because pessimism is usually interpreted as an unhealthy psychological disposition or character flaw demanding a cure, rather than a serious perspective worth lending an ear to (Dienstag 2006). There is a more substantive objection to pessimism leveled by some radicals, who argue that pessimism is implicitly conservative (if not explicitly) and detached from praxis. For example, Lukács (1980) argues that Schopenhauer was unknowingly an apologist of capitalism's barbarism and the function of Schopenhauer's thought is to prevent its adherents in the intelligentsia from critically questioning and changing the social order and encouraging them, instead, to bask in existential nothingness as the real world collapsed around them.

Yet there is a pessimistic dimension in all genuinely radical thought. For example, is there any better definition of a pessimist than Eagleton's (1991: 82) memorable definition of a socialist: "someone who is unable to get over his or her astonishment that most people who have lived and died have spent lives of wretched, fruitless, unremitting toil"? Similarly, there is a radical dimension in all genuinely pessimistic thought. Horkheimer (2004) defends the *resistance* at the heart of pessimism and praises Schopenhauer as the "teacher for modern times" because he "enunciates the negative and preserves it in thought, thus exposing the motive for solidarity shared by men and all beings: their abandonment" (Horkheimer 1974: 81, 82). Adorno (1973a: 381) says that "nihilism" — when this word does not mean a callous disinterest in the world but, instead, the belief that the "created world is radically evil, and its negation is the chance of another world that is not yet" — has emancipatory moments and is better than cheap reassurances that life is as meaningful as you make it.

Further, there is a metaphysical point of agreement between the dialectic, in its materialist form, and atheistic strands of pessimism: an understanding that there is no inherent purpose to, or meaning in, existence and that human action is vain from the perspective of cosmic time and the colossal and constantly expanding universe. One outcome of materialism for dialectics is the haunting knowledge that even if humanity manages to create a better social world, it is still a biological species that will die and fade from memory.

> The student of the Enlightenment is convinced that the future generations for which he is fighting for are irrevocably transitory and that, in the end, nothingness is victorious over joy. Certainly he is inspired by the notion of a higher form of society and of a brighter existence for all human beings. However, the reason why he prefers personal engagement to conformity toward existing reality and a career lies not in a commandment or an inner voice pregnant with promises, but rather only in his wishes and desires, which will one day disappear. It may appear a noble goal for humans to live on this earth more happily and wisely than they did under the bloody and stultifying conditions that tend to designate the end of social life forms. However, the future generations will die out anyway, and the earth will continue its course as if nothing had happened. Skepticism and nihilism are speaking here. In reality, a sincere consciousness and honest action begin in the place where this simple truth gains ground and is resolutely retained. (Horkheimer 1993b: 158)

For dialectical thought, this knowledge neither encourages renunciation nor pseudo-spontaneous self-affirmation, both now caught in the webs of the culture industry. Pessimism remains static rather than dialectical unless the dual desires for life-affirmation and peace transform into an anticipatory longing for their future actualization. For example, there is an anticipatory reconciliation procured by the knowledge that all the pointless striving and senseless suffering of the world, including painful memories, will inevitably fade away. Is there any more reliable consolation than "This too shall pass," including the maxim's cosmic application? Like any thinking person, the dialectician, as much as the pessimist, grasps the incomparable solace in reflecting on the heat death of the universe. Yet, the restless dialectic resists the calm ossifying into complacency: perhaps even the consolation of knowing that entropy will win in the end is a form of alienated reconciliation, an echo of our social condition where "all pictures of reconciliation, peace, and quiet resemble the picture of death" so long as "the world is as it is" (Adorno 1973a: 381).

Like Adorno's (1967b; 1973a: 376ff) evaluation of Spengler and nihilism, one should seek out the truths of the pessimistic tradition without succumbing to its reified and often reactionary ideas, including pessimism's tendency to naturalize socially-produced suffering, pardon blind domination, ignore potentiality, and cast history into a fated process. For example, Schopenhauer is too optimistic because he promises the individual an escape from suffering (Horkheimer 1978: 218f). In truth, the individual is powerless in the face of the "negative absolute," and attempts to escape through resignation will end in self-deception (Adorno 1973a: 377) (e.g., see the discussion of mindfulness in chapter 2).

Too often, both Dionysian and renunciatory forms of pessimism share a common *fatalism*: reality is contemptible, but it cannot be changed—beyond perhaps, in Dionysian pessimism, what can be changed through heroic individual acts made possible by our ostensibly absolute and distressing freedom. This fatalism, which has begun to infect climate politics (see chapter 3), is the seat of pessimism's alienated reconciliation with reality, and rooted in reification: "This is all quite bad, but it could not be otherwise." The dialectic responds: "This is all quite bad, but there are alternatives, and, even if these alternatives are unlikely to actualize, they should be brought to consciousness and pursued as a collective."

The genuine spirit of pessimism, a negativity birthed by the "sight of the *evil and wickedness* in the world" (Schopenhauer 1958: 171), lives on in dialectics where pessimism, unable to stand the sight, terminates in the endorsement of individual self-actualization or renunciation. In dialectical thought, negativity manifests as social analysis and critique, slingshot back to Earth by anticipatory reconciliation.

> People to whom despair is not a technical term may ask whether it would be better for nothing at all to be than something. Not even to this is there a general answer. For a man in a concentration camp it would be better not to have been born—if one who escaped in time is permitted to venture any judgement about this. And yet the lighting up of an eye, indeed the feeble tail-wagging of a dog one gave a tidbit it promptly forgets, would make the ideal of nothingness evaporate. (Adorno 1973a: 380)

Adorno and related thinkers are not residents of Schopenhauer's "Grand Hotel Abyss" (Lukács 1971b: 9) in order to enjoy a nihilistically detached yet aesthetically pleasurable stay without mounting any real challenges to the miseries of the real world. Instead, they are paradoxically preserving a radical hope that, at one time, could genuinely manifest as optimism.

> When the doors are barricaded, it is doubly important that thought not be interrupted. It is rather the task of thought to analyse the reasons behind this situation and to draw the consequences from these reasons. ... If there is any chance of changing the situation, it is only through undiminished insight. (Adorno 1991: 173)

Keeping the causes of harm in constant gaze is the route to the potential discovery of historical alternatives. In more abstract theological terms, negativity is the remaining route to:

> contemplate all things as they would present themselves

from the standpoint of redemption. ... Perspectives must be fashioned that displace and estrange the world, reveal it to be, with its rifts and crevices, as indigent and distorted as it will appear one day in the messianic light. To gain such perspectives without velleity or violence, entirely from felt contact with its objects—this alone is the task of thought. It is the simplest of all things, because the situation calls imperatively for such knowledge, indeed because consummate negativity, once squarely faced, delineates the mirror-image of its opposite [i.e. utopia]. (Adorno 1978: 247)

In his most abstract formulation of the goal of reconciliation, Adorno (1973a: 389, cf. 2001: 170ff) says that Kant was right to place a block between knowledge and metaphysics in the present, due to our continued "imprisonment in self-preservation," but that Kant was dishonest to project this condition into the future (see Jarvis 1998: 208ff). A social product that reflects the resignation required in capitalist societies, Kant's block paradoxically suggests a "metaphysical mourning." The *possibility* of the transcendent—now a future transformation into a form of living that is not reduced to production and consumption for the sake of production and consumption— must always remain open. This remains true even though the best we can hope for is a less bad catastrophe.

Dialectics today requires a restlessness birthed by the knowledge that a less bad future is possible but unlikely to emerge, and holding that contradiction in consciousness without lapsing into fatalism, radical posturing, easy answers, techno-optimism, online shopping, and other forms of alienated reconciliation. This disappointing and possibly fruitless endeavor is not only kept afloat by a hope harnessed to the discovery of mere possibilities and experiences of mundane transcendence, but also nourished by the dialectic's very opposition to the status quo and desire to actualize the not-yet—its negativity.

References

Abromeit J (2016) Critical theory and the persistence of right-wing populism. *Logos* 15(2-3). http://logosjournal.com/2016-vol-15-nos-2-3/.

Adorno TW (1967a) A portrait of Walter Benjamin. In: *Prisms*. Cambridge: MIT Press, 227-241.

Adorno TW (1967b) Spengler after the decline. In: *Prisms*. Cambridge: MIT Press, 53-72.

Adorno TW (1973a) *Negative Dialectics*. New York: Continuum.

Adorno TW (1973b) *The Jargon of Authenticity*. Evanston, IL: Northwestern University Press.

Adorno TW (1977) Reconciliation under duress. In: Adorno TW, Benjamin W, Bloch E, Brecht B, and Lukács G, *Aesthetics and Politics*. New York: Verso, 151-176.

Adorno TW (1978) *Minima Moralia*. New York: Verso.

Adorno TW (1984) *Aesthetic Theory*. New York: Routledge & Kegan Paul.

Adorno TW (1991) Resignation. In Bernstein JM (ed) *The Culture Industry: Selected Essays on Mass Culture*. New York: Routledge, 171-175.

Adorno TW (1998) *Critical Models*. New York: Columbia University Press.

Adorno TW (2000a) *Introduction to Sociology*. Stanford: Stanford University Press.

Adorno TW (2000b) *Problems of Moral Philosophy*. Stanford: Stanford University Press.

Adorno TW (2001) *Kant's Critique of Pure Reason*. Stanford: Stanford University Press.

Adorno TW (2003a) Late capitalism or industrial society? In: Tiedemann R (ed) *Can One Live After Auschwitz? A Philosophical Reader*. Stanford: Stanford University Press, 111–125.

Adorno TW (2003b) Reflections on class theory. In: Tiedemann

R (ed) *Can One Live After Auschwitz? A Philosophical Reader.* Stanford: Stanford University Press, 93–110.

Adorno, TW (2006) *History and Freedom: Lectures 1964-1965.* Malden, MA. Polity Press.

Adorno TW and Horkheimer M (2011) *Towards a New Manifesto.* New York: Verso.

Alier JM (2009) Socially sustainable economic de-growth. *Development and Change* 40(6): 1099-1119.

Allen A (2016) *The End of Progress: Decolonizing the Normative Foundations of Critical Theory.* New York: Columbia University Press.

Allen M (2019) The problem with claiming we have "12 years to climate breakdown." *Real Clear Science.* https://www.realclearscience.com/articles/2019/04/24/the_problem_with_claiming_we_have_12_years_to_climate_breakdown.html.

Alston P (2019) Climate change and poverty: Report of the Special Rapporteur on extreme poverty and human rights. *United Nations Human Rights Council,* 25.

Althusser L (1971) Ideology and ideological state apparatuses. In: *Lenin and Philosophy and Other Essays.* New York: Monthly Review Press, 127-193.

Amsler SS (2015) *The Education of Radical Democracy.* London: Routledge.

Anderson B (2006) "Transcending without transcendence": Utopianism and an ethos of hope. *Antipode* 38(4): 691-710.

Anderson K and Bows A (2011). Beyond "dangerous" climate change: Emission scenarios for a new world. *Philosophical Transactions of the Royal Society A: Mathematical, Physical and Engineering Sciences* 369(1934): 20-44.

Anderson K and Bows A (2012) A new paradigm for climate change. *Nature Climate Change* 2(9): 639–640.

Anderson K and Bows-Larkin A (2013) Avoiding dangerous climate change demands degrowth strategies from wealthier nations. Kevin Anderson Blog. https://kevinanderson.info/

blog/avoiding-dangerous-climate-change-demands-de-growth-strategies-from-wealthier-nations/.

Antonio RJ (1981) Immanent critique as the core of critical theory: Its origins and developments in Hegel, Marx and contemporary thought. *British Journal of Sociology* 32(3): 330-345.

Antonio RJ and Clark B (2015) The climate change divide in social theory. In: Dunlap RE and Brulle RJ (eds) *Climate Change and Society: Sociological Perspectives*. New York: Oxford University Press.

Arias-Maldonado M (2019) Blooming landscapes? The paradox of utopian thinking in the Anthropocene. *Environmental Politics* DOI: 10.1080/09644016.2019.1703384.

Arzuaga F (2019). Socially necessary superfluity: Adorno and Marx on the crises of labor and the individual. *Philosophy & Social Criticism* 45(7): 819–843.

Baillie JB (1967) Note to "Freedom of self-consciousness." In: Hegel GWF *The Phenomenology of Mind*. New York: Harper Torchbooks, 241.

Barkham P (2018) 'We're doomed': Mayer Hillman on the climate reality no one else will dare mention. *The Guardian*. https://www.theguardian.com/environment/2018/apr/26/were-doomed-mayer-hillman-on-the-climate-reality-no-one-else-will-dare-mention.

Bauman Z (2001) Consuming life. *Journal of Consumer Culture* 1(1): 9-29.

Bauman Z (2003) *Liquid Love: On the Frailty of Human Bonds*. Malden, MA: Blackwell.

Baumann C (2011). Adorno, Hegel and the concrete universal. *Philosophy & Social Criticism* 37(1): 73-94.

Bayoumi M (2005) Reconciliation without duress: Said, Adorno, and the autonomous intellectual. *Alif* 25: 46-64.

Beiner R (1984) Walter Benjamin's philosophy of history. *Political Theory* 12(3): 423-434.

Benhabib S (1986) *Critique, Norm, and Utopia: A Study of the Foundations of Critical Theory*. New York: Columbia University Press.

Benjamin W (1968) Theses on the philosophy of history. In: *Illuminations*. New York: Schocken.

Berger P and Pullberg S (1965) Reification and the sociological critique of consciousness. *History and Theory* 4(2): 196-211.

Biro A (2005) *Denaturalizing Ecological Politics: Alienation from Nature from Rousseau to the Frankfurt School and Beyond*. Toronto: University of Toronto Press.

Biro A (2011) *Critical Ecologies: The Frankfurt School and Contemporary Environmental Crises*. Toronto: University of Toronto Press.

Bloch E (1968) Man as possibility. *CrossCurrents* 18(3): 273-283.

Bloch E (1971) *On Karl Marx*. New York: Herder and Herder.

Bloch E (1972) *Atheism in Christianity: The Religion of the Exodus and the Kingdom*. New York: Herder and Herder.

Bloch E (1976) Dialectics and hope. *New German Critique* 9: 3-10.

Bloch E (1986) *The Principle of Hope*. Cambridge, MA: MIT Press.

Blühdorn I (2007) Sustaining the unsustainable: Symbolic politics and the politics of simulation. *Environmental Politics* 16(2): 251-275.

Boldyrev I (2014) *Ernst Bloch and his Contemporaries: Locating Utopian Messianism*. New York: Bloomsbury.

Boucher O, Randall D, Artaxo P, Bretherton C, Feingold G, Forster P, Kerminen V-M, Kondo Y, Liao H, Lohmann U, Rasch P, Satheesh SK, Sherwood S, Stevens B, and Zhang XY (2013) Clouds and aerosols. In Stocker TF, Qin D, Plattner GK, Tignor M, Allen SK, Boschung J, Nauels A, Xia Y, Bex V, and Midgley PM (eds) *Climate Change 2013: The Physical Science Basis*. Cambridge and New York: Cambridge University Press.

Bourdieu P (1977) *Outline of a Theory of Practice*. New York: Cambridge University Press.

Bragman W and Colangelo M (2019) Kamala Harris's signature achievement was a complete failure. *Jacobin.* https://www. jacobinmag.com/2019/09/kamala-harris-back-on-track-program-prisons

Braverman, Harry. 1998. *Labor and Monopoly Capital: The Degradation of Work in the Twentieth Century.* New York: Monthly Review.

Bryson A, Ebbinghaus B, and Visser J (2011) Introduction: Causes, consequences and cures of union decline. *European Journal of Industrial Relations* 17(2): 97-105.

Buis A (2019) A degree of concern: Why global temperatures matter. Parts 1 and 2. National Aeronautics and Space Administration. https://climate.nasa.gov/news/2865/a-degree-of-concern-why-global-temperatures-matter/.

Bukharin N (1966) *The ABC of Communism.* Ann Arbor: University of Michigan Press.

Burgis B (2019, May 20) *Ben Burgis on Socialism and Social Democracy* [Video]. Zero Books. YouTube. https://www. youtube.com/watch?v=yFXvbUCw4hA.

Burgis B, Hamilton C, McManus M, and Trejo M (2020) *Myth and Mayhem: A Leftist Critique of Jordan Peterson.* Washington, DC: Zero Books.

Burke PJ, Shahiduzzaman M, and Stern DI (2015) Carbon dioxide emissions in the short run: The rate and sources of economic growth matter. *Global Environmental Change* 33: 109–121.

Burns JK (2015) Poverty, inequality and a political economy of mental health. *Epidemiology and Psychiatric Sciences* 24(2): 107-113.

Carter Z (2020) Democrats are handing Donald Trump the keys to the country. *Huffington Post.* https://www.huffpost.com/entry/senate-democrats-donald-trump-coronavirus-bill_n_5 e7b77a6c5b62a1870d62d83.

Case A and Deaton A (2015). Rising morbidity and mortality in midlife among white non-Hispanic Americans in the

21st century. *Proceedings of the National Academy of Sciences* 112(49): 15078-15083.

Case A and Deaton A (2017) Mortality and morbidity in the 21st century. *Brookings Papers on Economic Activity*, Spring 2017: 397-476.

Cassegård C and Thörn H (2018) Toward a postapocalyptic environmentalism? Responses to loss and visions of the future in climate activism. *Environment and Planning E* 1(4): 561-578.

Chrostowska SD (2013) Thought woken by memory: Adorno's circuitous path to utopia. *New German Critique* 40(1), 93-117.

Cioran E (1973) *The Trouble with Being Born*. New York: Seaver Books.

Clements R (2013) Marxism and the God question: Perspectives from the Frankfurt School. *The Other Journal* 22. https://theotherjournal.com/2013/07/22/marxism-and-the-god-question-perspectives-from-the-frankfurt-school/.

Climate Action Tracker (2019) Warming projections global update. Climate Analytics. https://climateactiontracker.org/documents/698/CAT_2019-12-10_BriefingCOP25_WarmingProjectionsGlobalUpdate_Dec2019.pdf

Cohen M (1994) *The Wager of Lucien Goldmann: Tragedy, Dialectics, and a Hidden God*. Princeton, NJ: Princeton University Press.

Collins C and Hoxie J (2018) Billionaire bonanza 2018: Inherited wealth dynasties of the United States. Institute for Policy Studies. Inequality.org. https://inequality.org/great-divide/billionaire-bonanza-2018-inherited-wealth-dynasties-in-the-21st-century-u-s/

Cook D (2008) Introduction. In Cook D (ed): *Theodor Adorno: Key Concepts*. Stocksfield, UK: Acumen, 41-46.

Cook D (2011) *Adorno on Nature*. New York: Routledge.

Corak M (2013) Income inequality, equality of opportunity, and intergenerational mobility. *Journal of Economic Perspectives* 27(3): 79-102.

Cox H (1970) Foreword. In Bloch E: *Man on His Own*. New York: Herder and Herder.

Cox C and Whalen M (2001) On evil: an interview with Alain Badiou. *Cabinet Magazine Online* 5. http://www.cabinetmagazine.org/issues/5/alainbadiou.php.

Curtin SC, Warner M, and Hedegaard H (2016) Increase in suicide in the United States, 1999-2014 (No. 2016). US Department of Health and Human Services, Centers for Disease Control and Prevention, National Center for Health Statistics.

Czeisler MÉ, Lane RI, Petrosky E, et al. (2020). Mental health, substance use, and suicidal ideation during the COVID-10 pandemic – United States, June 24-30, 2020. Centers for Disease Control and Prevention. Morbidity and mortality weekly report. https://www.cdc.gov/mmwr/volumes/69/wr/mm6932a1.htm.

Dahms H (1998) Beyond the carousel of reification: Critical social theory after Lukács, Adorno, and Habermas. *Current Perspectives in Social Theory* 18: 3-62.

D'Alisa G, Demaria F and Kallis G (eds) (2014) *Degrowth: A Vocabulary for a New Era*. New York: Routledge.

Darnoi DNK (1967) *The Unconscious and Eduard von Hartmann: A Historico-Critical Monograph*. The Hague, The Netherlands: Martinus Nijhoff.

Data for Progress (nd) The Green New Deal. https://www.dataforprogress.org/green-new-deal.

Dienstag JF (2006) *Pessimism: Philosophy, Ethic, Spirit*. Princeton, NJ: Princeton University Press.

Dietz T, Burns TR and Buttel FH (1990) Evolutionary theory in sociology: An examination of current thinking. *Sociological Forum* 5: 155-171.

Dietz T, Rosa EA, and York R (2012) Environmentally efficient well-being: Is there a Kuznets curve? Applied Geography 32(1): 21–28.

Doogan K (2001) Insecurity and long-term employment. *Work,*

Employment and Society 15(3): 419-441.

Drewnowski A and Specter SE (2004) Poverty and obesity: The role of energy density and energy costs. *The American Journal of Clinical Nutrition* 79(1): 6–16.

Dunphie CJ (1876) *The Splendid Advantages of Being a Woman and Other Erratic Essays.* New York: Lovell, Adam, Wesson, and Company.

Dupuy JP (2009) The precautionary principle and enlightened doomsaying: rational choice before the apocalypse. *Occasion* 1(1): 1-13.

Durkheim É (1938) *The Rules of Sociological Method.* New York: Free Press.

Durkheim É (1951) *Suicide: A Study in Sociology.* New York: Free Press.

Eagleton T (1991) *Ideology: An Introduction.* New York: Verso.

Eagleton T (2011) *Why Marx was Right.* New Haven: Yale University Press.

Eagleton T (2015) *Hope Without Optimism.* Charlottesville: University of Virginia Press.

Eagleton T (2016) Utopias, past and present: Why Thomas More remains astonishingly radical. *Utopian Studies* 27(3): 412-417.

Eckersley R (1992) Environmentalism and Political Theory: Toward an Ecocentric Approach. New York: SUNY Press.

Ekins E (2015) Poll: Americans like free markets more than capitalism and socialism more than a govt managed economy. *Reason.* https://reason.com/2015/02/12/poll-americans-like-free-markets-more-th/.

Featherstone L (2019) Radical academics for the status quo. *Jacobin.* https://jacobinmag.com/2019/12/radical-academics-judith-butler-kamala-harris-donation.

Feenberg A (1999) *Questioning Technology.* New York: Routledge.

Feenberg A (2005) *Heidegger and Marcuse: The Catastrophe and Redemption of History.* New York: Routledge.

Ferraro AJ, Highwood EJ and Charlton-Perez AJ (2014)

Weakened tropical circulation and reduced precipitation in response to geoengineering. *Environmental Research Letters* 9(1): 014001.

Fevre R (2007) Employment insecurity and social theory: the power of nightmares. *Work, Employment and Society* 21(3): 517-535.

Fisher M (2009) *Capitalist Realism: Is There No Alternative?* Washington, DC: Zero Books.

Fisher M (2013) Exiting the vampire castle. *openDemocracy.* https://www.opendemocracy.net/en/opendemocracyuk/exiting-vampire-castle/.

Fitzgerald JB, Jorgenson AK and Clark B (2015) Energy consumption and working hours: a longitudinal study of developed and developing nations, 1990-2008. *Environmental Sociology* 3(1): 213-223.

Forse RA and Krishnamurty DM (2015) Epidemiology and discrimination in obesity. In Nguyen NT, Blackston RP, Morton JM, Ponce J, and Rosenthal RJ (eds) *The ASMBS Textbook of Bariatric Surgery*, vol. 1. New York: Springer, 3-12.

Foster JB (2009) *The Ecological Revolution: Making Peace with the Planet.* New York: Monthly Review Press.

Foster JB (2018) There is still time for an ecological revolution to prevent Hothouse Earth. *Rebel News.* http://www.rebelnews.ie/2018/08/24/john-bellamy-foster-there-is still-time-for-an-ecological-revolution/.

Foster JB (2017) The long ecological revolution. *Monthly Review* 69(6). https://monthlyreview.org/2017/11/01/the-long-ecological-revolution/.

Foster JB (2019) Making war on the planet: Geoengineering and capitalism's creative destruction of the Earth. *Science for the People*, Special Issue: Geoengineering. https://magazine.scienceforthepeople.org/making-war-on-the-planet/.

Foster JB, Clark B, and York R (2010) *The Ecological Rift: Capitalism's War on the Earth.* New York: Monthly Review

Press.

Foster JB and Magdoff F (2009) *The Great Financial Crisis: Causes and Consequences*. New York: Monthly Review Press.

Foster JB and McChesney RW (2012) *The Endless Crisis: How Monopoly-Finance Capital Produces Stagnation and Upheaval from the USA to China*. New York: Monthly Review Press.

Foster JB and McChesney RW (2014) Surveillance capitalism: Monopoly-finance capital, the military industrial complex, and the digital age. *Monthly Review* 66(3). https://doi.org/10.14452/MR-066-03-2014-07_1.

Frank T (2016) *Listen, Liberal: Or, What Ever Happened to the Party of the People?* New York: Metropolitan Books.

Frase P (2011) Four futures. *Jacobin*. https://www.jacobinmag.com/2011/12/four-futures/

Frase P (2016) Social democracy's breaking point. *Jacobin*. https://www.jacobinmag.com/2016/06/social-democracy-polanyi-great-transformation-welfare-state/.

Fraser N (2017) The end of progressive neoliberalism. *Dissent*. https://www.dissentmagazine.org/online_articles/progressive-neoliberalism-reactionary-populism-nancy-fraser.

Fraser N (2019) *The Old is Dying and the New Cannot Be Born: From Progressive Neoliberalism to Trump and Beyond*. New York: Verso Books.

Franzen J (2019) What if we stopped pretending? *The New Yorker*. https://www.newyorker.com/culture/cultural-comment/what-if-we-stopped-pretending.

Freud S (1961) *Civilization and Its Discontents*. New York: W. W. Norton and Company.

Freyenhagen F (2013) *Adorno's Practical Philosophy: Living Less Wrongly*. New York: Cambridge University Press.

Fromm E (1955) *The Sane Society*. Greenwich, CT: Premier.

Fromm E (1966) *You Shall Be as Gods*. Greenwich: Fawcett.

Fromm E (1968) *The Revolution of Hope: Toward a Humanized*

Technology. New York: Bantam.

Fromm E (1973) *The Anatomy of Human Destructiveness*. New York: Fawcett Crest.

Frisk L and Nynäs P (2012) Characteristics of contemporary religious change: Globalization, neoliberalism, and interpretative tendencies. In: Nynäs P, Lassander M, and Utriainen T (eds) *Post-Secular Society*. New York: Routledge, 47-70.

Gaby S and Caren, N (2016) The rise of inequality: How social movements shape discursive fields. *Mobilization* 21(4): 413-429.

Global Carbon Budget (2019) An annual update of the global carbon budget and trends. Available from: https://www. globalcarbonproject.org/carbonbudget/index.htm.

Giridharadas A (2018) *Winners Take All: The Elite Charade of Changing the World*. New York: Borzoi.

Goldmann L (1964) *The Hidden God: A Study of Tragic Vision in the Pensées of Pascal and the Tragedies of Racine*. London: Routledge and Kegan Paul.

Goldstein WS (2001) Messianism and Marxism: Walter Benjamin and Ernst Bloch's dialectical theories of secularization. *Critical Sociology* 27(2): 246-281.

Goldstein WS (2005) The dialectics of religious rationalization and secularization: Max Weber and Ernst Bloch. *Critical Sociology* 31(1-2): 115-151.

Gordon PE (2016) *Adorno and Existence*. Cambridge, MA: Harvard University Press.

Gorz A (1967) *Strategy for Labor*. Boston: Beacon Press.

Gowan P (2017) A plan to win. *Jacobin*. https://www.jacobinmag. com/2017/11/social-democracy-sweden-meidner-plan-socialism.

Gowan P (2018a) A plan to nationalize fossil fuel companies. *Jacobin*. https://jacobinmag.com/2018/03/nationalize-fossil-fuel-companies-climate-change.

Gowan P (2018b) The radical reformist. *Jacobin*. https://
jacobinmag.com/2018/03/rudolf-meidner-sweden-social-
democracy-labor

Gramsci A (1971) *Selections from the Prison Notebooks*. New York:
International Publishers.

Greenfield A (2017) *Radical Technologies: The Design of Everyday
Life*. New York: Verso.

Griner D (2017) 18 bullish stats about the state of US advertising.
Adweek. https://www.adweek.com/agencies/18-bullish-stats-
about-the-state-of-u-s-advertising/.

Gunderson R (2014) Problems with the defetishization thesis:
Ethical consumerism, alternative food systems, and
commodity fetishism. *Agriculture and Human Values* 31(1):
109-117.

Gunderson R (2015a) A defense of the "Grand Hotel Abyss":
The Frankfurt School's nonideal theory. *Acta Sociologica*
58(1): 25-38.

Gunderson R (2015b) Environmental sociology and the Frankfurt
School 1: Reason and capital. *Environmental Sociology* 1(3):
224-235.

Gunderson R (2016) Environmental sociology and the
Frankfurt School 2: Ideology, techno-science, reconciliation.
Environmental Sociology 2(1): 64-76.

Gunderson R (2017) Ideology critique for the environmental
social sciences: What reproduces the treadmill of production?
Nature and Culture 12(3): 263-289.

Gunderson R (2018) Degrowth and other quiescent futures:
Pioneering proponents of an idler society. *Journal of Cleaner
Production*, *198*, 1574-1582.

Gunderson R (2020) *Making the Familiar Strange: Sociology Contra
Reification*. New York: Routledge.

Gunderson R, Stuart D, and Petersen B (2019) The political
economy of geoengineering as plan B: Technological
rationality, moral hazard, and new technology. *New Political*

Economy 24(5): 696-715.

Gunderson R, Stuart D, Petersen B, and Yun S-J (2018) Social conditions to better realize the environmental gains of alternative energy: Degrowth and collective ownership. *Futures* 99: 36-44.

Guthman J (2007) Commentary on teaching food: Why I am fed up with Michael Pollan et al. *Agriculture and Human Values* 24(2): 261-264.

Gur-Ze'ev I (1998) Walter Benjamin and Max Horkheimer: From utopia to redemption. *Journal of Jewish Thought and Philosophy* 8: 119-155.

Habermas J (1973) *Legitimation Crisis*. Boston: Beacon Press.

Habermas J (1979) Consciousness-raising or redemptive criticism: The contemporaneity of Walter Benjamin. *New German Critique* 17: 30-59.

Habermas J (1987) *The Theory of Communicative Action,* vol. 2: *Lifeworld and System: A Critique of Functionalist Reason.* Boston: Beacon Press.

Haffner S (2013) Failure of a revolution: Germany 1918-1919. Plunkett Lake Press. https://libcom.org/files/Failure%20 of%20a%20Revolution_%20German%20-%20Sebastian%20 Haffner.pdf.

Hagopian A, Flaxman AD, Takaro TK, Al Shatari SAE, Rajaratnam J, Becker S, ... and Murray CJ (2013) Mortality in Iraq associated with the 2003–2011 war and occupation: findings from a national cluster sample survey by the university collaborative Iraq Mortality Study. *PLoS Med* 10(10): e1001533.

Hamel L, Norton M, Pollitz K, Levitt L, Claxton G, and Brodie M (2016) The burden of medical debt: Results from the Kaiser Family Foundation/New York Times medical bills survey. Kaiser Family Foundation. https://www.kff. org/report-section/the-burden-of-medical-debt-section-3-consequences-of-medical-bill-problems/.

Handelman S (1991) Walter Benjamin and the angel of history. *Cross Currents* 41(3): 344-352.

Hardesty L (2015) Finger-mounted reading device for the blind. *MIT News*. http://news.mit.edu/2015/finger-mounted-reading-device-blind-0310.

Harlan SL, Pellow DN, Roberts JT, Bell SE, Holt WG, and Nagel J (2015) In: Dunlap RE and Brulle RJ (eds) Climate Change and Society: Sociological Perspectives. New York: Oxford University Press, 127-163.

Harrington A (2001) New German aesthetic theory. *Radical Philosophy* 109. https://www.radicalphilosophy.com/article/new-german-aesthetic-theory.

Harvey D (2005) *A Brief History of Neoliberalism*. New York: Oxford University Press.

Harvey D (2014) *Seventeen Contradictions and the End of Capitalism*. New York: Oxford University Press.

Harvey D (2019) "The neoliberal project is alive but has lost its legitimacy": David Harvey. *The Wire*. https://thewire.in/economy/david-harvey-marxist-scholar-neo-liberalism.

Hedges C (2018) *America: The Farewell Tour*. New York: Simon and Schuster.

Hegel GWF (1956) *The Philosophy of History*. New York: Dover.

Hegel GWF (1967) *The Phenomenology of Mind*. New York: Harper Torchbooks.

Hegel GWF (1976) *Philosophy of Right*. London: Oxford University Press.

Hegel, GWF (2010) The Science of Logic. New York: Cambridge University Press.

Hickel J (2019) Degrowth: A theory of radical abundance. Real-World Economic Review 87: 54–68.

Hickel J and Kallis G (2019) Is green growth possible? New Political Economy. DOI: 10.1080/13563467.2019.1598964.

Hickel J (2019) Bill Gates says poverty is decreasing. He couldn't be more wrong. *The Guardian*. https://www.theguardian.

com/commentisfree/2019/jan/29/bill-gates-davos-global-poverty-infographic-neoliberal.

Hill K (2020) The secretive company that might end privacy as we know it. *New York Times*. https://www.nytimes.com/2020/01/18/technology/clearview-privacy-facial-recognition.html.

Hohendahl PU (2013) Progress revisited: Adorno's dialogue with Augustine, Kant, and Benjamin. *Critical Inquiry* 40(1): 242-260.

Holpuch A (2020) Louisiana court upholds black man's life sentence for trying to steal hedge clippers. *The Guardian*. https://www.theguardian.com/us-news/2020/aug/07/lousiana-court-denies-life-sentence-appeal-fair-wayne-bryant-black-man-hedge-clippers.

Honneth A (1994) The social dynamics of disrespect: On the location of critical theory today. *Constellations* 1(2): 255-269.

Horkheimer M (1947) *Eclipse of Reason*. New York: Continuum.

Horkheimer M (1972) *Critical Theory: Selected Essays*. New York: Continuum.

Horkheimer M (1973). Foreword. In: Jay M *The Dialectical Imagination*. Boston: Little, Brown.

Horkheimer M (1974) Schopenhauer today. In: *Critique of Instrumental Reason: Lectures and Essays Since the End of World War II*. New York: Continuum.

Horkheimer M (1978) Dawn & Decline. New York: Seabury Press.

Horkheimer M (1993a) Materialism and morality. In: *Between Philosophy and Social Science: Selected Early Writings*. Cambridge: MIT Press, 15-47.

Horkheimer M (1993b) Remarks on philosophical anthropology. In: *Between Philosophy and Social Science: Selected Early Writings*. Cambridge: MIT Press, 151-175.

Horkheimer M (2004) Schopenhauer and society (1955). *Qui Parle* 15(1): 85-96.

Horkheimer M and Adorno TW (1969) *Dialectic of Enlightenment.* New York: Continuum.

Horton J (1964) The dehumanization of anomie and alienation: A problem in the ideology of sociology. *The British Journal of Sociology* 15(4): 283-300.

Houseman T (2013) Auschwitz as eschaton: Adorno's negative rewriting of the messianic in critical theory. *Millennium* 42(1): 155-176.

Hollenbeck JE (2016) Interaction of the role of concentrated animal feeding operations (CAFOs) in emerging infectious diseases (EIDS). *Infection, Genetics and Evolution* 38: 44-46.

Hood M (2019) Earth warming more quickly than thought, new climate models show. *Phys.org.* https://phys.org/news/2019-09-earth-quickly-climate.html.

Hudson W (1982) *The Marxist Philosophy of Ernst Bloch.* New York: St. Martin's Press.

Inequality.org (2020) Wealth inequality in the United States. https://inequality.org/facts/wealth-inequality/.

Intergovernmental Panel on Climate Change (IPCC) (2014) *Climate Change 2014: Synthesis Report. Contribution of Working Groups I, II and III to the Fifth Assessment Report of the Intergovernmental Panel on Climate Change.* IPCC. Geneva, Switzerland.

Intergovernmental Panel on Climate Change (IPCC) (2018) Summary for policymakers. In: *Global warming of 1.5°C.* World Meteorological Organization, Geneva, Switzerland. Available at: http://www.people-press.org/2015/01/15/ (accessed 19 November 2018).

International Energy Agency (2019) World Energy Outlook. https://webstore.iea.org/world-energy-outlook-2019.

Jacobs M. (2013) Green growth. In: Falkner R (ed) *Handbook of Global Climate and Environmental Policy.* Malden, MA: Wiley-Blackwell, 197-214.

Jacoby R (1981) *Dialectic of Defeat: Contours of Western Marxism.*

New York: Cambridge University Press.

Jacoby R (1999) *The End of Utopia: Politics and Culture in an Age of Apathy*. New York: Basic Books.

Jacoby R (2005) *Picture Imperfect: Utopian Thought for an Anti-Utopian Age*. New York: Columbia University Press.

James W (1961) *The Varieties of Religious Experience: A Study in Human Nature*. New York: Collier Books.

Jameson F (2003) Future city. *New Left Review* (21): 65-80.

Jameson F (2004) The politics of utopia. *New Left Review* 25: 35-54.

Jameson F (2005) *Archaeologies of the Future: The Desire Called Utopia and Other Science Fictions*. New York: Verso.

Jarvis S (1998) *Adorno: A Critical Introduction*. New York: Routledge.

Jay M (1973) *The Dialectical Imagination*. Boston, MA: Little, Brown and Company.

Jay M (1984) *Marxism & Totality: The Adventures of a Concept from Lukács to Habermas*. Berkeley: University of California Press.

Jay M (2016) *Reason After Its Eclipse: On Late Critical Theory*. Madison, WI: University of Wisconsin Press.

Johanisova N and Wolf S (2012) Economic democracy: A path for the future? *Futures* 44(6): 562-570.

Johnston J (2008) The citizen-consumer hybrid: Ideological tensions and the case of Whole Foods Market. *Theory & Society* 37(3): 229-270.

Johnson P (2008). Social philosophy. In: Cook D (ed.) *Theodor Adorno: Key concepts*. Stocksfield, UK: Acumen.

Jonna RJ and Foster JB (2016) Marx's theory of working-class precariousness: It's relevance today. *Monthly Review* 67. https://monthlyreview.org/2016/04/01/marxs-theory-of-working-class-precariousness/.

Jorgenson AK and Clark B (2012) Are the economy and the environment decoupling? A comparative international study, 1960-2005. *American Journal of Sociology* 118(1): 1–44.

Jütten T (2010) What is reification? A critique of Axel Honneth.

Inquiry 53(3): 235–256.

Kalleberg AL (2011) *Good Jobs, Bad Jobs: The Rise of Polarized and Precarious Employment Systems in the United States, 1970s-2000s.* New York: Russell Sage Foundation.

Kallis G (2011) In defence of degrowth. *Ecological Economics* 70(5): 873-880.

Kallis G (2019) Socialism without growth. *Capitalism Nature Socialism* 30(2): 189-206.

Kautsky K (1910) *The Class Struggle (Erfurt Program).* Chicago: Charles H. Kerr & Company.

Keith DW (2013) *A Case for Climate Engineering.* Cambridge, MA: MIT Press.

Kellner D and O'Hara H (1976) Utopia and Marxism in Ernst Bloch. *New German Critique* 9: 11-34.

Kerbo HR (2012) *Social Stratification and Inequality: Class Conflict in Historical, Comparative, and Global Perspective,* 8th edn. New York: McGraw-Hill.

Kingsnorth P (2010) Why I stopped believing in environmentalism and started the Dark Mountain project. *The Guardian.* https://www.theguardian.com/environment/2010/apr/29/environmentalism-dark-mountain-project.

Klein N (2015) *This Changes Everything: Capitalism vs. the Climate.* New York: Simon and Schuster.

Klein N (2019) *On Fire: The (Burning) Case for a Green New Deal.* New York: Simon and Schuster.

Knight KW, Rosa EA, and Schor JB (2013) Could working less reduce pressures on the environment? A cross-national panel analysis of OECD countries, 1970–2007. *Global Environmental Change* 23(4): 691-700.

Knight KW and Schor JB (2014) Economic growth and climate change: A cross-national analysis of territorial and consumption-based carbon emissions in high-income countries. Sustainability 6(6): 3722–3731.

Kojève A (1969) *Introduction to the Reading of Hegel: Lectures on the Phenomenology of Spirit*. Ithaca, NY: Cornell University Press.

Kołakowski L (2005) *Main Currents of Marxism: The Founders, the Golden Age, the Breakdown*. New York: W. W. Norton & Company.

Kovel J (2018) Therapy in late capitalism. In: Tweedy R (ed) *The Political Self: Understanding the Social Context for Mental Illness*. New York: Routledge, 43-67.

Krasnoff L (2008) *Hegel's Phenomenology of Spirit: An Introduction*. New York: Cambridge University Press.

Kunze C and Becker S (2015) Collective ownership in renewable energy and opportunities for sustainable degrowth. *Sustainability Science* 10(3): 425-437.

Lasch C (1991) *The True and Only Heaven: Progress and Its Critics*. New York: W. W. Norton & Company.

Lauer Q (1993) *A Reading of Hegel's Phenomenology of Spirit*. New York: Fordham University Press.

Leiss W (1974) The Domination of Nature. New York: Braziller.

Lent J (2018) Steven Pinker's ideas about progress are fatally flawed. These eight graphs show why. *Resilience*. https://patternsofmeaning.com/2018/05/17/steven-pinkers-ideas-about-progress-are-fatally-flawed-these-eight-graphs-show-why/.

Lerner AJ (2015) *Redemptive Hope: From the Age of Enlightenment to the Age of Obama*. New York: Fordham University Press.

Levitas R (1990) Educated hope: Ernst Bloch on abstract and concrete utopia. *Utopian Studies* 1(2): 13-26.

Levitas R and Sargisson L (2003) Utopia in dark times: Optimism/pessimism and utopia/dystopia. In: Baccolini R and Moylan T (eds) *Dark Horizons*. New York: Routledge, 13-28.

Levitz E (2019) Jonathan Franzen's climate pessimism is justified. His fatalism is not. *Intelligencer*. https://nymag.com/intelligencer/2019/09/what-jonathan-franzen-gets-wrong-about-climate-change.html.

Levy Z (1997) Utopia and reality in the philosophy of Ernst Bloch. In: Owen J and Moylan T (eds) *Not Yet: Reconsidering Ernst Bloch*. New York: Verso, 175-185.

Lewis R (2015) As UN says world to warm by 3 degrees, scientists explain what that means. *Al Jazeera*. Available from: http://america.aljazeera.com/articles/2015/9/23/climate-change-effects-from-a-3-c-world.html.

Lohmann L (2005) Marketing and making carbon dumps: Commodification, calculation and counterfactuals in climate change mitigation. *Science as Culture* 14(3): 203–235.

Löwy M (1992) *Redemption and Utopia: Jewish Libertarian Thought in Central Europe: A Study of Elective Affinity*. London: Athlone Press.

Lukács G (1971a) *History and Class Consciousness*. Cambridge: MIT Press.

Lukács G (1971b) *The Theory of the Novel*. London: Merlin Press.

Lukács G (1980) The bourgeois irrationalism of Schopenhauer's metaphysics. In: Fox M (ed) *Schopenhauer: His Philosophical Achievement*. New Jersey: Barnes and Nobel Books, 183-93.

Luke T (2020) *Anthropocene Alerts: Critical Theory of the Contemporary as Ecocritique*. New York: Telos Press.

Lund C, Breen A, Flisher AJ, Kakuma R, Corrigall J, Joska JA, ... and Patel V (2010) Poverty and common mental disorders in low and middle income countries: A systematic review. *Social Science & Medicine* 71(3): 517-528.

Luthar SS (2003) The culture of affluence: Psychological costs of material wealth. *Child Development* 74(6): 1581-1593.

Luthar SS and Becker BE (2003) Privileged but pressured? A study of affluent youth. *Child Development* 73(5): 1593-1610.

MacFarquhar L (2015) *Strangers Drowning: Impossible Idealism, Drastic Choices, and the Urge to Help*. New York: Penguin.

Macy J and Johnstone C (2012) *Active Hope: How to Face the Mess We're in Without Going Crazy*. Novato, CA: New World Library.

Magdoff F and Williams C (2017) *Creating an Ecological Society: Toward a Revolutionary Transformation*. New York: Monthly Review Press.

Malm A (2018) Marx on steam: From the optimism of progress to the pessimism of power. *Rethinking Marxism* 30(2): 166-185.

Marcetic B (2017) The two faces of Kamala Harris. *Jacobin*. https://www.jacobinmag.com/2017/08/kamala-harris-trump-obama-california-attorney-general.

Marcuse H (1955) *Eros and Civilization*. New York: Vintage.

Marcuse M (1960) *Reason and Revolution: Hegel and the Rise of Social Theory*. Boston: Beacon.

Marcuse H (1964) *One-Dimensional Man*. Boston: Beacon.

Marcuse H (1968) Negations. Boston: Beacon.

Marcuse H (1969) *An Essay on Liberation*. Boston: Beacon.

Marcuse H (1970) The end of utopia. In: *Five Lectures*. Boston: Beacon, 62-82.

Marcuse H (1972) *Counterrevolution and Revolt*. Boston: Beacon.

Marasco R (2015) *The Highway of Despair: Critical Theory after Hegel*. New York: Columbia University Press.

Marmot M, Ferrie J, Newman K, and Stansfeld S (2001) The contribution of job insecurity to socio-economic inequalities. Research findings: 11. Health Variations Programme.

Marshall R (2015) How many ads do you see in one day? *Red Crow Marketing Inc.* https://www.redcrowmarketing.com/2015/09/10/many-ads-see-one-day/.

Marwood D (2016) *Sur l'eau*, or how to read Adorno: Guy de Maupassant and the negative dialectic of utopia. *Modernism/modernity* 23(4): 833-854.

Marx K (1963) Contribution to the critique of Hegel's Philosophy of Right: Introduction. In: Bottomore TB (ed) *Karl Marx: Early Writings*. New York: McGraw-Hill, 41-59.

Marx K (1964) *The economic and philosophic manuscripts of 1844*. New York: International.

Marx K (1970) *A Contribution to the Critique of Political Economy.* New York: International Publishers.

Marx K (1973) *Grundrisse.* New York: Vintage.

Marx K (1976) *Capital,* vol. 1. New York: Vintage.

Marx K and Engels F (1977) *The German Ideology.* New York: International Publishers.

Matthews D (2020) A theory of mental health and monopoly capitalism. *Monthly Review* 71(10). https://monthlyreview.org/2020/03/01/a-theory-of-mental-health-and-monopoly-capitalism/

Mattick P (1972) *One-Dimensional Man in Class Society.* New York: Herder and Herder.

Mauss M (1967) *The Gift: Forms and Functions of Exchange in Archaic Societies.* New York: W. W. Norton and Company.

McCarney J (1990) *Social Theory and the Crisis of Marxism.* New York: Verso.

McCarthy MA (2018) Democratic socialism isn't social democracy. *Jacobin.* https://jacobinmag.com/2018/08/democratic-socialism-social-democracy-nordic-countries.

Mendens-Flohr PR (1983) "To brush history against the grain": The eschatology of the Frankfurt School and Ernst Bloch. *Journal of the American Academy of Religion* 51(4): 631-650.

Mendieta E (ed) (2005) *The Frankfurt School on Religion: Key Writings by the Major Thinkers.* New York: Routledge.

Merikangas KR, He JP, Burstein M, Swanson SA, Avenevoli S, Cui L, Benjet C, Georgiades K, and Swendsen J (2010) Lifetime prevalence of mental disorders in US adolescents: Results from the National Comorbidity Survey Replication—Adolescent Supplement (NCS-A). *Journal of the American Academy of Child & Adolescent Psychiatry.* 49(10): 980-989.

Meštrović SG (1991) *The Coming Fin de Siècle: An Application of Durkheim's Sociology to Modernity and Postmodernity.* London: Routledge.

Michaels WB (2010) Identity politics: A zero-sum game. *New*

Labor Forum. https://newlaborforum.cuny.edu/2010/11/06/identity-politics-a-zero-sum-game/.

Miliband R, Saville J, Liebman M, and Panitch L (eds) (1985/1986) *Social Democracy and After. Socialist Register* 22.

Millennium Ecosystem Assessment (2005) *Ecosystems and Human Well-being: Synthesis.* Island Press, Washington, DC.

Mills PJ (1991) Feminism and ecology: On the domination of nature. Hypatia 6(1): 162–78.

Mitchell NS, Catenacci VA, Wyatt HR, and Hill JO (2011) Obesity: Overview of an epidemic. *Psychiatric Clinics* 34(4): 717-732.

Molarius A, Seidell JC, Sans S, Tuomilehto J, and Kuulasmaa K (2000) Educational level, relative body weight, and changes in their association over 10 years: An international perspective from the WHO MONICA Project. *American Journal of Public Health* 90(8): 1260–1268.

Monbiot G (2016) Neoliberalism is creating loneliness. That's what's wrenching society apart. *The Guardian.* https://www.theguardian.com/commentisfree/2016/oct/12/neoliberalism-creating-loneliness-wrenching-society-apart.

Monroe R (2019) #Vanlife, the bohemian social-media movement. *The New Yorker.* https://www.newyorker.com/magazine/2017/04/24/vanlife-the-bohemian-social-media-movement.

Moore TJ and Mattison DR (2017) Adult utilization of psychiatric drugs and differences by sex, age, and race. *JAMA Internal Medicine* 177(2): 274-275.

Mussell S (2013) "Pervaded by a chill": The dialectic of coldness in Adorno's social theory. *Thesis Eleven* 117(1): 55-67.

Muûls M, Colmer J, Martin R, and Wagner U (2016) Evaluating the EU Emissions Trading System: Take it or leave it? An assessment of the data after ten years. Grantham Institute Briefing Paper 21. Imperial College London.

Nagle A (2017) *Kill All Normies: Online Culture Wars from 4chan and Tumblr to Trump and the Alt-Right.* Washington, DC: Zero Books.

National Institution on Drug Abuse (2019) Overdose death rates. https://www.drugabuse.gov/related-topics/trends-statistics/overdose-death-rates.

National Institute of Mental Health (2019) Mental illness. https://www.nimh.nih.gov/health/statistics/mental-illness.shtml.

Nelson ES (2011) Revisiting the dialectic of environment: Nature as ideology and ethics in Adorno and the Frankfurt School. *Telos* 155: 105–126.

Ng K (2015) Ideology critique from Hegel and Marx to critical theory. *Constellations* 22(3): 393-404.

Nielsen Global Connect (2018) Time flies: US adults now spend nearly half a day interacting with media. https://www.nielsen.com/us/en/insights/article/2018/time-flies-us-adults-now-spend-nearly-half-a-day-interacting-with-media/.

Nietzsche F (1967) *The Birth of Tragedy and The Case of Wagner.* New York: Vintage.

Nietzsche F (1974) *The Gay Science.* New York: Vintage.

Norton MI and Ariely D (2011) Building a better America — One wealth quintile at a time. *Perspectives on Psychological Science* 6(1): 9-12.

Obach BK (2004) New labor: Slowing the treadmill of production? *Organization & Environment* 17(3): 337-354.

O'Connor B (2008) Philosophy of history. In: Cook D (ed) *Theodor Adorno: Key Concepts.* Stocksfield, UK: Acumen, 179-195.

Organization for Economic Co-operation and Development (OECD) (2011) *Towards Green Growth.* OECD: Paris.

Ott MR (2006) The notion of the totally "other" and its consequence in the critical theory of religion and the rational choice theory of religion. In: Goldstein WS (ed) *Marx, Critical Theory, and Religion: A Critique of Rational Choice.* Boston: Brill, 121-150.

Ott K (2018) On the political economy of solar radiation

management. *Frontiers in Environmental Science* 6: 43.

Oxfam International (2017) An economy for the 99%. Oxfam. https://www.oxfam.org/en/research/economy-99.

Palley TI (2012) *From Financial Crisis to Stagnation: The Destruction of Shared Prosperity and the Role of Economics.* New York: Cambridge University Press.

Peters M (2014) *Schopenhauer and Adorno on Bodily Suffering: A Comparative Analysis.* New York: Palgrave Macmillan.

Peterson J (2018) *12 Rules for Life: An Antidote to Chaos.* Toronto: Penguin Random House.

Piketty T (2020) *Capital and Ideology.* Cambridge, MA: Harvard University Press.

Pinkard T (1994) Hegel's *Phenomenology: The Sociality of Reason.* New York: Cambridge University Press.

Pinker S (2018). *Enlightenment Now: The Case for Reason, Science, Humanism, and Progress.* New York: Penguin.

Prádanos LI (2018) *Postgrowth Imaginaries: New Ecologies and Counterhegemonic Culture in Post-2008 Spain.* Liverpool, UK: Liverpool University Press.

Pullinger M (2014) Working time reduction policy in a sustainable economy: Criteria and options for its design. *Ecological Economics* 103: 11-19.

Purser RE (2019) *McMindfulness: How Mindfulness Became the New Capitalist Spirituality.* London: Repeater.

Reed A (2018a) Antiracism: A neoliberal alternative to a left. *Dialectical Anthropology* 42(2): 105-115.

Reed A (2018b) Black politics after 2016. *nonsite.org.* https://nonsite.org/article/black-politics-after-2016.

Richerson PJ and Boyd R (2005) *Not by Genes Alone: How Culture Transformed Human Evolution.* Chicago: University of Chicago Press.

Ricoeur P (2004) *Memory, History, Forgetting.* Chicago: University of Chicago Press.

Rideout VJ, Foehr UG, and Roberts DF (2010) Generation

M²: Media in the lives of 8- to 18-year-olds. Kaiser Family Foundation. https://www.kff.org/wp-content/ uploads/2013/04/8010.pdf.

Rieff D (2016) *In Praise of Forgetting: Historical Memory and Its Ironies*. New Haven: Yale University Press.

Roberts D (2011) The brutal logic of climate change. *Grist*. https://grist.org/climate-change/2011-12-05-the-brutal-logic-of-climate-change/.

Robinson NJ (2019) *Why You Should Be a Socialist*. New York: All Points.

Robock A (2008a) Geoengineering: It's not a Panacea. *Geotimes* 53(7): 58-58.

Robock A (2008b) 20 reasons why geoengineering may be a bad idea. *Bulletin of the Atomic Scientists* 64(2): 14-18.

Robock A, Marquardt A, Kravitz B, and Stenchikov G (2009) Benefits, risks, and costs of stratospheric geoengineering. *Geophysical Research Letters* 36: 1-9.

Robock A, Bunzl M, Kravitz B, and Stenchikov GL (2010) A test for geoengineering? *Science* 327(5965): 530-531.

Rosnick D (2013) Reduced work hours as a means of slowing climate change. *Real-World Economic Review* 63: 124-133.

Rosnick D and Weisbrot M (2006) Are shorter working hours good for the environment? A comparison of US and European Energy consumption. Center for Economic and Policy Research. Washington, DC.

Rousseau J-J (1992) *The Reveries of the Solitary Walker*. Indianapolis, IN: Hackett Publishing.

Sachs J (2020) The huge divide between Biden and Sanders. *CNN*. https://www.cnn.com/2020/03/11/opinions/biden-sanders-democratic-primary-generations-sachs/index.html.

Sanders B (nd) The Green New Deal. Bernie Sanders Official Campaign Website. https://berniesanders.com/en/issues/green-new-deal/.

Schechter A (2018) Why democracy fails to reduce inequality:

Blame the Brahmin left. *Promarket*. https://promarket. org/2018/04/17/democracy-fails-reduce-inequality-blame-brahmin-left/.

Schopenhauer A (1958) *The World as Will and Representation,* vol 2. New York: Dover.

Schopenhauer A (1969) *The World as Will and Representation*, vol. 1. New York: Dover.

Schopenhauer A (1974) *Parerga and Paralipomena*, vol. 2. Oxford: Clarendon Press.

Schor JB (2005) Sustainable consumption and worktime reduction. *Journal of Industrial Ecology* 9(1-2): 37-50.

Schor JB (2014) *Born to Buy: The Commercialized Child and the New Consumer Cult*. New York: Simon and Schuster.

Schor JB and Jorgenson AK (2019) Is it too late for growth? *Review of Radical Political Economics* 51(2): 320-329.

Schwartz JM and Sunkara B (2017) Social democracy is good. But not good enough. *Jacobin*. https://jacobinmag.com/2017/08/ democratic-socialism-judis-new-republic-social-democracy-capitalism.

Schwartz O (2020) My journey into the dark, hypnotic world of a millennial guru. *The Guardian*. https://www.theguardian. com/world/2020/jan/09/strange-hypnotic-world-millennial-guru-bentinho-massaro-youtube.

Scranton R (2018) *We're Doomed. Now What? Essays on War and Climate Change*. New York: Soho Press.

Sekulova F (2015) Happiness. In: D'Alisa G, Demaria F and Kallis G (eds) *Degrowth: A Vocabulary for a New Era*. New York: Routledge, 113-116.

Shaw D, Newholm T and Dickinson R (2006) Consumption as voting: An exploration of consumer empowerment. *European Journal of Marketing* 40(9/10): 1049-1067.

Sheehan J (2010) The fat acceptance movement. *Everyday Health*. https://www.everydayhealth.com/weight/the-fat-accep tance-movement.aspx.

Silverman J (2017) Privacy under surveillance capitalism. *Social Research* 84(1): 147-164.

Skirke C (2020) After Auschwitz. In: Gordon PE, Hammer E and Pensky M (eds) *A Companion to Adorno*. Hoboken, NJ: John Wiley & Sons, 567-582.

Skocpol T (1979) *States and Social Revolutions: A Comparative Analysis of France, Russia, and China*. New York: Cambridge University Press.

Sobal J and Stunkard AJ (1989) Socioeconomic status and obesity: A review of the literature. *Psychological Bulletin* 105: 260–275.

Solomon M (1972) Marx and Bloch: Reflection on utopia and art. *Telos* 13: 68-85.

Solty I (2020) Max Horkheimer, a teacher without a class. *Jacobin*. https://www.jacobinmag.com/2020/02/max-horkheimer-frankfurt-school-adorno-working-class-marxism.

Spencer H (1921) *The Principles of Sociology*, vol. 2. New York: D. Appleton and Company.

Standing G (2011) *The Precariat: The New Dangerous Class*. London: Bloomsbury.

Steffen W, Richardson K, Rockström J, Cornell SE, Fetzer I, Bennett EM, … and Folke C (2015) Planetary boundaries: Guiding human development on a changing planet. *Science* 347(6223): 1259855.

Steffen W, Rockström J, Richardson K, Lenton TM, Folke C, Liverman D, …. and Schellnhuber HJ (2018) Trajectories of the Earth System in the Anthropocene. *Proceedings of the National Academy of Sciences* 115(33): 8252-8259.

Stern N (2006) *Stern Review on the Economics of Climate Change*. New York: Cambridge University Press.

Stevenson H and Dryzek JS (2014) *Democratizing Global Climate Governance*. New York: Cambridge University Press.

Stone A (2008) Adorno and logic. In: Cook D (ed) *Theodor Adorno: Key Concepts*. Stocksfield, UK: Acumen, 47-62.

Stoner AM and Melathopoulos A (2015) *Freedom in the Anthropocene: Twentieth-Century Helplessness in the Face of Climate Change*. New York: Palgrave Macmillan.

Stoner AM and Melathopoulos A (2016) If climate "changes everything," why does so much remain the same? *Logos* 15(1). http://logosjournal.com/2016/stoner/.

Streeck W (2016). *How Will Capitalism End? Essays on a Failing System*. New York: Verso.

Stuart D (In review) Radical hope: Truth, virtue ethics, and hope for what is left in Extinction Rebellion.

Stuart D, Gunderson R and Petersen B (2020a) *Climate Change Solutions: Beyond the Capital-Climate Contradiction*. Ann Arbor: University of Michigan Press.

Stuart D, Gunderson R and Petersen B (2020b) *The Degrowth Alternative: A Path to Address our Environmental Crisis?* New York: Routledge.

Substance Abuse and Mental Health Services Administration (2018) 2017 NSDUH Annual National Report. https://www.samhsa.gov/data/report/2017-nsduh-annual-national-report.

Sullivan C (2007) What's the point of secret gigs? *The Guardian*. https://www.theguardian.com/music/musicblog/2007/may/16/foreditorssecretgigs.

Sunkara B (2019). *The Socialist Manifesto: The Case for Radical Politics in an Era of Extreme Inequality*. New York: Basic Books.

Surprise K (2018) Preempting the second contradiction: Solar geoengineering as spatiotemporal fix. *Annals of the American Association of Geographers* 108(5): 1228-1244.

Sverke M, Hellgren J and Näswall K (2002) No security: A meta-analysis and review of job insecurity and its consequences. *Journal of Occupational Health Psychology* 7(3): 242-264.

Swenson-Lengyel W (2017) Beyond eschatology: Environmental pessimism and the future of human hoping. *Journal of Religious Ethics* 45(3): 413-436.

Tar Z (1977) *The Frankfurt School: The Critical Theories of Max*

Horkheimer and Theodor W. Adorno. New York: Wiley.

Terreblanche SJ (2008) On history and salvation in Emmanuel Levinas and Ernst Bloch. *HTS Teologiese Studies* 64(2): 885-906.

Tettlebaum M (2008) Political philosophy. In: Cook D (ed) *Theodor Adorno: Key Concepts.* Stocksfield, UK: Acumen, 131-146.

Thomä D (2012) Passion lost, passion regained: How Arendt's anthropology intersects with Adorno's theory of the subject. In: Rensmann L and Gandesha S (eds) *Arendt and Adorno: Political and Philosophical Investigations.* Stanford: Stanford University Press.

Thompson MJ (2016) *The Domestication of Critical Theory.* Lanham, MD: Rowman and Littlefield.

Thompson P (2016) Ernst Bloch and the spirituality of utopia. *Rethinking Marxism* 28(3-4): 438-452.

Thompson P and Žižek S (2013) *The Privatization of Hope: Ernst Bloch and the Future of Utopia.* Durham, NC: Duke University Press.

Thorlakson T, de Zegher JF, and Lambin EF (2018) Companies' contribution to sustainability through global supply chains. *Proceedings of the National Academy of Sciences* 115(9): 2072-2077.

Toffler A (1970) *Future Shock.* New York: Bantam.

Traverso E (2017) *Left-Wing Melancholia: Marxism, History, and Memory.* New York: Columbia University Press.

Turner B (2001) Peter Berger. In: Elliot A and Turner BS (eds) *Profiles in Contemporary Social Theory.* Thousand Oaks, CA: Sage, 107-116.

Tweedy R (2017) A mad world: Capitalism and the rise of mental illness. *Red Pepper.* https://www.redpepper.org.uk/a-mad-world-capitalism-and-the-rise-of-mental-illness/.

Uetricht M and Day M (2020) *Bigger Than Bernie: How We Go from the Sanders Campaign to Democratic Socialism.* New York:

Verso.

Unamuno A (1972) *The Tragic Sense of Life in Men and Nations.* Princeton, NJ: Princeton University Press.

United Nations Framework Convention on Climate Change (2015) The Paris Agreement. Available at: https://unfccc. int/process-and-meetings/the-paris-agreement/the-paris-agreement.

US National Research Council (2015) *Climate Intervention: Reflecting Sunlight to Cool Earth.* Committee on Geoengineering Climate: Technical Evaluation and Discussion of Impacts. Board on Atmospheric Sciences and Climate. Ocean Studies Board. Division on Earth and Life Studies. The National Academies Press: Washington, DC.

Verhaeghe P (2014) *What About Me? The Struggle for Identity in a Market-Based Society.* London: Scribe.

Vogel S (1996) *Against Nature: The Concept of Nature in Critical Theory.* New York: SUNY Press.

von Hartmann E (1931) *Philosophy of the Unconscious: Speculative Results According to the Inductive Method of Physical Science.* London: W. Stewart & Co.

Wallace-Wells D (2017) The uninhabitable Earth. *Intelligencer.* https://nymag.com/intelligencer/2017/07/climate-change-earth-too-hot-for-humans.html.

Wallace-Wells D (2019a) The cautious case for climate optimism. *Intelligencer.* https://nymag.com/intelligencer/2019/02/book-excerpt-the-uninhabitable-earth-david-wallace-wells.html.

Wallace-Wells D (2019b) We're getting a clearer picture of the climate future—and it's not as bad as it once looked. *Intelligencer.* https://nymag.com/intelligencer/2019/12/climate-change-worst-case-scenario-now-looks-unrealistic.html.

Weber M (1946) *From Max Weber: Essays in Sociology.* New York: Oxford University Press.

Whitebook J (1979) The problem of nature in Habermas. *Telos*

40: 41-69.

Wilde O (1915) *The Soul of Man Under Socialism*. Portland, ME: Thomas B. Mosher.

Wilkinson R and Pickett K (2011) *The Spirit Level: Why Greater Equality Makes Societies Stronger*. New York: Bloomsbury.

Williams B (2016) Why baby boomers don't get Bernie Sanders. *The New Republic*. https://newrepublic.com/article/130220/baby-boomers-dont-get-bernie-sanders.

Winnick M and Zolna R (2016) Putting a finger on our phone obsession — Mobile touches: A study on humans and their tech. dScout. https://blog.dscout.com/mobile-touches.

Wolff EN (2017) Household wealth trends in the United States, 1962 to 2016: Has middle class wealth recovered? National Bureau of Economic Research. Working Paper No. 24085.

Wolin R (1980) An aesthetic of redemption: Benjamin's path to *Trauerspiel*. *Telos* 43: 61-90.

Wong KLX and Dobson AS (2019) We're just data: Exploring China's social credit system in relation to digital platform ratings cultures in Westernised democracies. *Global Media and China* 4(2): 220-232.

World Bank (2012) *Inclusive Green Growth: The Pathway to Sustainable Development*. World Bank, Washington, DC.

World Bank (2014) *Turn Down the Heat: Why a 4°C Warmer World Must be Avoided*. http://documents.worldbank.org/curated/en/865571468149107611/Turn-down-the-heat-why-a-4-C-warmer-world-must-be-avoided.

World Inequality Lab (2018) World inequality report. https://wir2018.wid.world/.

World Wildlife Federation (2016) Living planet report. https://www.worldwildlife.org/pages/living-planet-report-2016.

Worthen J (1999) Remembrance and redemption: Including Walter Benjamin. *Theology* 102(808): 262-270.

Wright C and Nyberg D (2015) *Climate Change, Capitalism, and Corporations: Processes of Creative Self-Destruction*. New York:

Cambridge University Press.

Wright EO (2010) *Envisioning Real Utopias*. Verso, New York.

Wyatt SB, Winters KP, and Dubbert PM (2006) Overweight and obesity: Prevalence, consequences, and causes of a growing public health problem. *The American Journal of the Medical Sciences* 331(4): 166-174.

York R (2010) The paradox at the heart of modernity: The carbon efficiency of the global economy. *International Journal of Sociology* 40(2): 6-22.

York R and Bell SE (2019) Energy transitions or additions? Why a transition from fossil fuels requires more than the growth of renewable energy. *Energy Research & Social Science* 51: 40-43.

York R and Clark B (2007) The problem with prediction: Contingency, emergence, and the reification of projections. *The Sociological Quarterly* 48(4): 713-743.

York R and Mancus P (2009) Critical human ecology: Historical materialism and natural laws. *Sociological Theory* 27(2): 122-149.

York R and McGee J (2016) Understanding the Jevons paradox. *Environmental Sociology* 2(1): 77-87.

York R, Rosa EA, and Dietz T (2003) Footprints on the earth: The environmental consequences of modernity. *American Sociological Review* 68(2): 279–300.

Young G (1976) The fundamental contradiction of capitalist production. *Philosophy & Public Affairs* 5(2): 196-234.

Young IM (2001) *Inclusion and Democracy*. New York: Oxford University Press.

Zitner A, Chinni D, and McGill B (2016) How Hillary won: How Hillary Clinton overcame the challenge from Sen. Bernie Sanders. *Wall Street Journal*. http://graphics.wsj.com/elections/2016/how-clinton-won/.

Žižek S (1989) *The Sublime Object of Ideology*. New York: Verso.

Žižek S (2005) Revenge of global finance. *In These Times*. https://

inthesetimes.com/article/2122/revenge_of_global_finance

Žižek S (2007) The liberal utopia: Part II: The market mechanism for the race of devils. *Lacan dot com.* http://www.lacan.com/zizliberal2.htm.

Žižek S (2011) *Living in the End Times.* New York: Verso.

Žižek S (2016) The seeds of imagination. In: Jameson F (ed) *An American Utopia.* New York: Verso.

Žižek S (2018) Why do people find Jordan Peterson convincing? Because the left doesn't have its own house in order. *Independent.* https://www.independent.co.uk/voices/jordan-peterson-clinical-psychologist-canada-popularity-convincing-why-left-wing-alt-right-cathy-a8208301.html.

Zuboff S (2015) Big other: Surveillance capitalism and the prospects of an information civilization. *Journal of Information Technology* 30(1): 75-89.

Zuboff S (2019) *The Age of Surveillance Capitalism: The Fight for a Human Future at the New Frontier of Power.* London: Profile Books.

Author Biography

Ryan Gunderson is an Associate Professor in the Department of Sociology and Gerontology at Miami University.

CULTURE, SOCIETY & POLITICS

The modern world is at an impasse. Disasters scroll across our smartphone screens and we're invited to like, follow or upvote, but critical thinking is harder and harder to find. Rather than connecting us in common struggle and debate, the internet has sped up and deepened a long-standing process of alienation and atomization. Zer0 Books wants to work against this trend. With critical theory as our jumping off point, we aim to publish books that make our readers uncomfortable. We want to move beyond received opinions.

Zer0 Books is on the left and wants to reinvent the left. We are sick of the injustice, the suffering and the stupidity that defines both our political and cultural world, and we aim to find a new foundation for a new struggle.

If this book has helped you to clarify an idea, solve a problem or extend your knowledge, you may want to check out our online content as well. Look for Zer0 Books: Advancing Conversations in the iTunes directory and for our Zer0 Books YouTube channel.

Popular videos include:

Žižek and the Double Blackmain

The Intellectual Dark Web is a Bad Sign

Can there be an Anti-SJW Left?

Answering Jordan Peterson on Marxism

Follow us on Facebook
at https://www.facebook.com/ZeroBooks and Twitter at https://twitter.com/Zer0Books

Bestsellers from Zer0 Books include:

Give Them An Argument
Logic for the Left
Ben Burgis
Many serious leftists have learned to distrust talk of logic. This is
a serious mistake.
Paperback: 978-1-78904-210-8 ebook: 978-1-78904-211-5

Poor but Sexy
Culture Clashes in Europe East and West
Agata Pyzik
How the East stayed East and the West stayed West.
Paperback: 978-1-78099-394-2 ebook: 978-1-78099-395-9

An Anthropology of Nothing in Particular
Martin Demant Frederiksen
A journey into the social lives of meaninglessness.
Paperback: 978-1-78535-699-5 ebook: 978-1-78535-700-8

In the Dust of This Planet
Horror of Philosophy vol. 1
Eugene Thacker
In the first of a series of three books on the Horror of Philosophy,
In the Dust of This Planet offers the genre of horror as a way of
thinking about the unthinkable.
Paperback: 978-1-84694-676-9 ebook: 978-1-78099-010-1

The End of Oulipo?
An Attempt to Exhaust a Movement
Lauren Elkin, Veronica Esposito
Paperback: 978-1-78099-655-4 ebook: 978-1-78099-656-1

Capitalist Realism
Is There No Alternative?
Mark Fisher
An analysis of the ways in which capitalism has presented itself
as the only realistic political-economic system.
Paperback: 978-1-84694-317-1 ebook: 978-1-78099-734-6

Rebel Rebel
Chris O'Leary
David Bowie: every single song. Everything you want to know,
everything you didn't know.
Paperback: 978-1-78099-244-0 ebook: 978-1-78099-713-1

Kill All Normies
Angela Nagle
Online culture wars from 4chan and Tumblr to Trump.
Paperback: 978-1- 78535-543-1 ebook: 978-1-78535-544-8

Cartographies of the Absolute
Alberto Toscano, Jeff Kinkle
An aesthetics of the economy for the twenty-first century.
Paperback: 978-1-78099-275-4 ebook: 978-1-78279-973-3

Malign Velocities
Accelerationism and Capitalism
Benjamin Noys
Long listed for the Bread and Roses Prize 2015, *Malign Velocities*
argues against the need for speed, tracking acceleration
as the symptom of the ongoing crises of capitalism.
Paperback: 978-1-78279-300-7 ebook: 978-1-78279-299-4

Meat Market
Female Flesh under Capitalism
Laurie Penny
A feminist dissection of women's bodies as the fleshy fulcrum of
capitalist cannibalism, whereby women are both consumers and
consumed.
Paperback: 978-1-84694-521-2 ebook: 978-1-84694-782-7

Babbling Corpse
Vaporwave and the Commodification of Ghosts
Grafton Tanner
Paperback: 978-1-78279-759-3 ebook: 978-1-78279-760-9

New Work New Culture
Work we want and a culture that strengthens us
Frithjoff Bergmann
A serious alternative for mankind and the planet.
Paperback: 978-1-78904-064-7 ebook: 978-1-78904-065-4

Romeo and Juliet in Palestine
Teaching Under Occupation
Tom Sperlinger
Life in the West Bank, the nature of pedagogy and the role of a
university under occupation.
Paperback: 978-1-78279-637-4 ebook: 978-1-78279-636-7

Ghosts of My Life
Writings on Depression, Hauntology and Lost Futures
Mark Fisher
Paperback: 978-1-78099-226-6 ebook: 978-1-78279-624-4

Sweetening the Pill
or How We Got Hooked on Hormonal Birth Control
Holly Grigg-Spall
Has contraception liberated or oppressed women?
Sweetening the Pill breaks the silence on the dark side of hormonal
contraception.
Paperback: 978-1-78099-607-3 ebook: 978-1-78099-608-0

Why Are We The Good Guys?
Reclaiming Your Mind from the Delusions of Propaganda
David Cromwell
A provocative challenge to the standard ideology that Western
power is a benevolent force in the world.
Paperback: 978-1-78099-365-2 ebook: 978-1-78099-366-9

The Writing on the Wall
On the Decomposition of Capitalism and its Critics
Anselm Jappe, Alastair Hemmens
A new approach to the meaning of social emancipation.
Paperback: 978-1-78535-581-3 ebook: 978-1-78535-582-0

Enjoying It
Candy Crush and Capitalism
Alfie Bown
A study of enjoyment and of the enjoyment of studying. Bown
asks what enjoyment says about us and what we say about
enjoyment, and why.
Paperback: 978-1-78535-155-6 ebook: 978-1-78535-156-3

Color, Facture, Art and Design
Iona Singh
This materialist definition of fine-art develops guidelines for
architecture, design, cultural-studies and ultimately social
change.
Paperback: 978-1-78099-629-5 ebook: 978-1-78099-630-1

Neglected or Misunderstood
The Radical Feminism of Shulamith Firestone
Victoria Margree
An interrogation of issues surrounding gender, biology,
sexuality, work and technology, and the ways in which our
imaginations continue to be in thrall to ideologies of maternity
and the nuclear family.
Paperback: 978-1-78535-539-4 ebook: 978-1-78535-540-0

How to Dismantle the NHS in 10 Easy Steps (Second Edition)
Youssef El-Gingihy
The story of how your NHS was sold off and why you will have
to buy private health insurance soon. A new expanded second
edition with chapters on junior doctors' strikes and government
blueprints for US-style healthcare.
Paperback: 978-1-78904-178-1 ebook: 978-1-78904-179-8

Digesting Recipes
The Art of Culinary Notation
Susannah Worth
A recipe is an instruction, the imperative tone of the expert, but
this constraint can offer its own kind of potential. A recipe need
not be a domestic trap but might instead offer escape – something
to fantasise about or aspire to.
Paperback: 978-1-78279-860-6 ebook: 978-1-78279-859-0

Most titles are published in paperback and as an ebook.
Paperbacks are available in traditional bookshops. Both print and
ebook formats are available online.
Follow us on Facebook
at https://www.facebook.com/ZeroBooks
and Twitter at https://twitter.com/Zer0Books